Hawk
Medicine

Hawk Medicine

H.J. Lewis

Vanwell Publishing Limited
St. Catharines, Ontario

Vanwell Publishing acknowledges the financial support of the
Government of Canada through the Book Publishing Industry
Development Program for our publishing activities.

Vanwell Publishing acknowledges the Government of Ontario
through the Ontario Media Development Corporation's Book
Initiative.

Vanwell Publishing Limited
P.O. Box 2131, 1 Northrup Crescent
St. Catharines, ON
Canada L2R 7S2
sales@vanwell.com
1-800-661-6136

Produced and designed by Tea Leaf Press Inc.
www.tealeafpress.com

Cover images:
Hawk: Stolz, Gary M./USFWS; Lightning: C. Clark/NOAA
Photo Library, NOAA Central Library; OAR/ERL/National
Severe Storms Laboratory (NSSL); Youth: PictureQuest

Printed in Canada

National Library of Canada Cataloguing in Publication

Lewis, Jane, 1971-
        Hawk medicine / H.J. Lewis.

ISBN 1-55068-113-3

        I. Title.

PS8573.E9764H38 2003   C813'.6   C2003-905466-7

For Virginia Campbell—
I'm so glad you're a part of my family.

Chapter One

Connor Smith stared out at the dark sky. Rain was tapping steadily against the classroom window. It was a good rhythm. Connor drummed his fingers quietly on his desk, keeping time with the rain.

"Mr. Smith!"

Connor stopped drumming. He looked up to see his teacher, Mr. Lowen, standing beside him.

"Sir?" Connor said.

"Perhaps you are in the wrong classroom," Mr. Lowen said loudly. "You seem to think this is music class."

A few kids snickered. Connor ran one hand over his cropped, dark hair. He looked Mr. Lowen in the eye and waited.

"Please keep in mind that this is English class and that your desk is not a musical instrument. Do I make myself clear?"

"Yes, sir," Connor said. He didn't apologize. It was only the second week of September. He was still new at the school, and he didn't want to show any weakness. The other kids would never leave him alone if he did. Connor had moved around a lot. He had been "the new kid" enough times to know the rules. It was the same at every school.

Mr. Lowen walked to the front of the classroom. "I hope you've all finished reading the short story I assigned. I like to make sure my students take their homework seriously. That's why, every once in a while, I give pop quizzes." He picked up a stack of papers from his desk and held them in the air.

There were a few loud groans throughout the classroom.

Suddenly, a huge crack of thunder split the air, rattling the windows. The girl sitting in front of Connor jumped. She quickly looked over her shoulder and gave Connor an embarrassed smile. Connor looked away and pretended not to notice.

Ashling Kerr was the best-looking girl in grade eleven. At least, that was Connor's opinion. And he would keep that opinion to himself. Ashling was dating Troy Sellers, and

Troy Sellers was not someone Connor wanted to mess with.

Luckily, Connor's assigned seat in English class was right behind Ashling. He could look at her (or at least the back of her head) and no one would notice. She had long, straight, reddish-brown hair. Today, it was in a ponytail. Ashling seemed really nice, too, even though Connor had never really talked to her.

Outside the window, lightning streaked across the sky.

"Take one and pass the rest back," said Mr. Lowen. He handed quizzes to the students at the front of the class.

The papers reached Ashling's desk. She turned and handed some to Connor. Their fingers touched, and an electric shock zapped between them. Ashling's light green eyes widened in surprise. She gave Connor a half-smile and shook her fingers. Then she quickly turned around again.

Lightning flashed again, followed by another loud crack of thunder. The lights flickered off and on.

"Mr. Lowen!" someone called. "We can't have a test if there's a power failure."

"If there is a power failure, Karl, I will postpone the test. For now, let's carry on." Mr. Lowen looked around the room. "You have ten minutes."

"Ten minutes?" a girl asked. "That's not enough time to write a test!"

"You now have nine minutes and forty-five seconds," said Mr. Lowen.

Connor quickly filled in the multiple-choice quiz. He quietly drummed on his knee with one hand and listened to the rain outside.

When the time was up, the students passed their papers forward. Connor handed a stack of quizzes to Ashling. Their fingers touched again, and Connor felt another zap. Ashling gave him a funny look.

"It's because of the storm," Connor mumbled. Ashling ignored him and turned around in her seat.

Suddenly, Connor wanted to go home. He was sick of this stupid school and not talking to anybody. He was sick of being new and not having any friends. There was no point in making friends, either, because his mom would just end up moving again at the end of the year. Maybe even before that.

At least this was the last class of the day. Connor sighed and stared out the window. The rhythm of the rain had changed—it was slower, lighter. The sound of it seemed to drown out the homework assignment Mr. Lowen was giving out.

When the bell rang, Connor was the first one out the door.

Troy Sellers was waiting for Ashling in the hall, holding some books and a football. He was a big guy—just the right size for a linebacker. Troy was telling a crude joke to the beefy-looking guy standing next to him. His friend grunted with laughter and slapped Troy on the back.

What is it about guys who play football? Connor wondered to himself. *Girls always seem to go for them, even if they're total jerks.*

Connor hated football. Basketball, now *that* was a real sport. Connor was built for it— he was tall, strong, and quick on his feet. Unfortunately, he couldn't try out for the team. He had to get an after-school job instead. Once he started working, he wouldn't have much time for practices or games.

Sometimes Connor hated his life.

The rain had stopped by the time he got outside. He avoided puddles as he walked to the bike rack. It took him a few minutes to open the rusty lock on his mountain bike.

By the time he was ready to go, crowds of students were coming out the front doors of the school. Connor spotted Ashling and Troy, so he ducked down and pretended to check his front tire. He watched as the couple walked arm in arm through the parking lot to Troy's red sports car. Troy opened the passenger door for Ashling.

Connor stopped watching. *Some guys have all the luck,* he thought, shaking his head. *Would Ashling like me if I had a sports car?* he wondered. Connor was saving up to buy a good drum kit. *Maybe I should be saving up for a car instead. Maybe in a million years I'll have enough money to buy one.*

Troy's car screeched out of the parking lot and fishtailed onto the street.

Why don't you just focus on reality, Connor told himself angrily. He put on his helmet and backpack and hopped on his bike. At least his method of transportation kept him in really good shape.

He made his way out of the parking lot and rode slowly toward home. Connor was glad to get away from school, but the reality of going home was not appealing. His mom would be at work, so the house would be empty and quiet. Boxes were piled everywhere, even though they had moved in a few weeks ago. There would be a note on the table from his mom, telling him which frozen dinner to heat up.

Connor rode his bike for about ten minutes. He crossed a set of railway tracks and came to a crossroads at the edge of town. He started to turn left, the way he always went, but then he put on his brakes. If he went that way, he would be home in just a few minutes.

He looked straight ahead. A long, empty dirt road stretched out in front of him, leading into the countryside.

He kept going straight. Home, and reality, could wait.

The breeze felt fresh against Connor's face as he biked down the dirt road. The air had that sharp smell that comes after a thunderstorm. Patches of blue were appearing in the sky, and the remaining clouds had faded from dark to light gray. Connor's tires whizzed through patches of wet gravel. He felt lighter somehow, knowing that he wasn't going home right away.

Connor was still learning his way around the small town. He hadn't biked out this way before. There weren't many houses around, just a field of corn on one side and a lot of trees on the other.

Soon he came to a stop sign where the road crossed an even smaller dirt road. A faded green street sign read "River Road." A hand-painted sign was nailed to a nearby telephone pole. It read "Fresh Eggs" and had an arrow pointing to the right.

Connor decided to turn right, even though he wasn't planning to buy any fresh eggs. The side road was in worse shape than the main road. Connor had to slow down to avoid the rain-filled potholes.

Tall maples and pine trees lined both sides of the road. A dog was barking nearby. Connor could see a driveway up on the right. At the end of the driveway was a mailbox with a little red flag on top.

All of a sudden, he felt something swoosh past his ear. Connor's bike wobbled and he almost lost his balance. It was a huge hawk! It was flying so close that Connor could almost reach out and touch it.

He stared at the powerful bird. Its brown wings were outstretched as it glided on an air current. The feathers on its chest and underbelly were white. The hawk was flying low, right in front of Connor. Then it beat its wings again and turned sharply, flying past the mailbox and up the driveway.

Connor was so busy watching the hawk that he forgot to watch the road. His front tire went into a deep pothole. The bike kicked up and he grabbed the handlebars hard. The next thing he knew, he was lying flat on his face. His bike was lying next to the mailbox, with one tire spinning in the air.

Connor groaned out loud. His knee was throbbing. He could feel the imprint of every little piece of gravel on the palms of his hands.

A dog barked. Connor looked up and saw a small black-and-white dog bounding down the driveway. It ran up to him and began sniffing his face. Connor decided not to make any sudden moves. The dog was small, but that didn't mean it had no teeth.

Connor felt its rough tongue on his cheek. "Yeeech!" He quickly wiped his face with his sleeve. *This is farm country*, he thought. *Who knows what that dog licked before it got to me?*

The dog sat down next to Connor. It started barking its head off.

"Shhhh," said Connor. "I'm all right." He sat up slowly and shrugged off his backpack.

The dog barked even louder.

Connor heard footsteps coming down the driveway. He stood up in a hurry, feeling like an idiot. "Nice. Sixteen years old and I fall off my bike," he mumbled to himself. His face stung.

An old man was walking toward him. He was wearing a faded, blue plaid jacket and big rubber boots. The man snapped his fingers and the dog stopped barking. He looked at the dirt on Connor's clothes and the bike lying on its side.

"Are you all right?" the man asked. His eyes were blue and friendly, and his face was full of wrinkles.

"Yeah, I'm okay," said Connor. "I wasn't watching where I was going." He brushed gravel off his jeans.

"Can you get home all right?" the man asked, looking at Connor's bike. "You could come up to the house and call someone if you need to."

Yeah, right, thought Connor. *You look like a harmless old geezer, but you could be a total psycho. You could have dead bodies in your basement. I'm not going anywhere near your house, thank you very much.*

"No, thanks. I'm really okay," Connor said politely.

"Well, at least let's get the dirt off your face." The man pulled a white handkerchief out of his pocket. "You can't go home looking like that, or you'll give your parents a fright." He dabbed at Connor's chin.

"Ow," Connor said before he could stop himself. He didn't bother to explain that he only had one parent.

The man handed Connor the cloth. "It'll be easier if you do it yourself. You've got dirt there and there." He pointed to Connor's chin and cheek.

Connor wiped his face. Dirt and blood came off on the handkerchief. The dog came over and licked Connor's leg.

The old man chuckled. "Don't mind little Biscuit, there. She's just trying to help."

Connor looked down at the dog. "Your dog's name is Biscuit?" he asked.

"It sure is," the man replied. He winked. "Her mother and grandmother were called Biscuit, too. Makes it easy for an old man to remember."

He walked over and picked up Connor's bike. He straightened the wheel and squeezed each tire. Then he wheeled it over to Connor. "Looks like it's still in one piece," he said.

"Thanks," said Connor, handing back the handkerchief. "I'd better get home."

The dog stopped licking Connor's leg. She sat down beside Connor's backpack and gave a little bark.

"Don't forget your bag," said the old man. He snapped his fingers and Biscuit trotted over to sit at his feet.

Connor picked up his backpack. A huge feather was sitting on the ground next to it. It was marked with brown and white stripes.

"Oh, look there." The man bent down and picked up the feather. "That's a hawk feather. Must be meant for you." He held it out to Connor.

"Um, thanks." Connor took the feather and stuck it in the top of his backpack. Then he got on his bike.

"Ride safely now," said the old man. He walked over to the mailbox and took out a few letters. Then he turned down the little red flag on top of the box. For the first time, Connor noticed the name painted on the side of the mailbox: SMITH.

As he biked back down River Road, he thought about old Mr. Smith. When Connor was little, he thought that he was related to everyone who had the last name "Smith." He thought that he was part of one huge family. Then he grew up and found out that there were thousands of people named Smith, and he wasn't related to any of them. Except his mom, of course.

His dad, wherever he was, wasn't a Smith. Connor's mom had never changed her last name. His dad hadn't stuck around long enough to marry her. He took off when she got pregnant with Connor.

Connor didn't even have grandparents. His mom's parents died before Connor was born. He had no grandparents, no aunts, no uncles, no cousins. Nobody.

He biked into town and turned onto his street: Linden Lane. Most of the houses on the street were small, and they were built really close to one another. One house had a bunch of old cars and car parts on the front lawn. It looked like a car graveyard. Across the road, two big guys were sitting on motorcycles, revving their engines. Connor biked quickly past that house, feeling like a wuss on his mountain bike.

By the time he got home, the streetlights were coming on. Connor's little white house looked dark and lonely. A pile of empty cardboard boxes sat in the driveway. He locked up his bike and went inside.

His first stop was his bedroom. It was a small room with not much furniture. His bed was just a mattress on the floor. A scratched-up, mismatched set of drums sat in the corner. Free weights lay scattered on the floor.

A quick look in the mirror told him that his face was going to look rough tomorrow. He had a scrape across one cheek and another on his chin. His knee was banged up, too, but it wasn't bad. His clothes were wrecked. He changed into warm-up pants and a T-shirt.

Connor picked up dirty laundry from the floor of his room. The washing machine was in the kitchen by the back door. He started the load of laundry and then checked the fridge. *Crap, out of milk again,* he thought. He filled a big glass with water from the tap.

A note from his mom was stuck to the fridge. *Honey, there's a meat pie in the freezer for dinner. Bake one hour at 350°. Don't forget to turn off the oven.*

What does she think, I'm four years old? Connor thought to himself. He knew how to use the oven. Not that it mattered—he couldn't wait an hour to eat dinner. He made three peanut butter sandwiches instead and took them into the living room.

Connor ate in front of the TV, using a cardboard box as a table. He wished his mom would finish unpacking soon. At their last house, she had never even bothered to unpack all the boxes.

They seemed to move almost every year. His mom always said that they had to move because she had a good job opportunity in another town. But the jobs never seemed to work out for very long.

She promised Connor that this time would be different. She had lived in this town before, when she was younger. She was moving back because her old friend Gina had offered her a job as a hostess at a fancy restaurant. Connor's mom figured she would make decent money there.

Connor thought about asking his mom if they could stay here for a couple of years. Just until he finished high school. *Would that be so much to ask?*

He stood up and turned off the TV. The washing machine had finished its load. Connor took out his laundry and hung it up outside on the clothesline. *I hope it doesn't rain again,* he thought, looking at the sky.

He went to his bedroom and dumped his books out of his backpack. *What was I supposed to do for English homework?* he wondered. He couldn't remember.

Connor flipped open his biology textbook. A sea of words and diagrams stared up at him. *Boring,* he thought.

He looked at his drums. *I'd better play now,* he decided, *before Mom gets home.* Homework could wait. Connor put on his favorite Shane Philips CD, then sat down and drummed along with the music.

The bedroom disappeared. Connor was on stage with the band. Lights were flashing; the crowd was cheering. People were dancing and waving their arms to the music. He drummed for hours. He was the best drummer this band had ever seen.

"Connor! Connor! Connor!" the crowd chanted.

Suddenly, the music stopped. "Connor! Are you listening to me?"

Connor looked up to see his mom standing beside his CD player. "Oh, hi Mom," he said.

His mom shook her head in mock frustration and smiled. "Hi, sweetheart."

Her smile faded when she saw Connor's face. "What happened to you?" she asked. "Did you get into a fight at school?"

"No," Connor said. "I just fell off my bike, like an idiot."

"Oh!" She reached out and gently touched his chin. "Does it hurt? Did you put antiseptic on it?"

Connor pushed her hand away. "I'm fine, Mom. Don't worry."

"I have something that will make you feel better," she said. "A piece of triple chocolate fudge cake from the restaurant. There was only one piece left, and they let me take it home."

"Thanks, but I'm not hungry. Besides, I don't want to get zits. My face looks bad enough right now, thanks to the gravel road I wiped out on."

His mom frowned. "Where were you riding your bike?"

"Out in the country. You know, that road just after the railroad tracks."

She gave him a worried look. "Connor, I don't want you riding out there," she said.

Connor decided not to mention that he had talked to a strange old man, too. "Okay, whatever, Mom," he said.

"I'm serious," she said. "It's not…safe."

"All right, already," Connor said.

She reached over and ruffled his hair. "Did you do your homework?"

"I was just about to start it."

His mom smiled and closed his bedroom door. Two seconds later, she opened it again.

"Oh, Connor, I almost forgot. I brought home a newspaper. I think there are some jobs listed that you could apply for."

"I'll look at it in the morning, okay Mom?" Connor said.

"Sure, sweetie. Get your homework done." She left the room.

Connor got ready for bed. He lay down on his mattress and opened his biology textbook. The book opened to a page that showed a diagram of a bird. Connor remembered the hawk feather and got it from his backpack.

It was a pretty cool feather. He twirled it around in his fingers while he did his assigned reading. When he was finished, he put the book and the feather beside his bed and turned out the light.

That night, he had his first nightmare.

Chapter Two

Thunder growled. The hawk was flying into the black clouds of the thunderstorm. Suddenly, the sky started to spin. The wind began to howl and the howling turned to screaming. Darkness, spinning, and screaming. The world was out of control.

Connor sat up in bed, terror pounding through his body. His legs were twisted up in the sheets. He quickly kicked free, as though he had been trapped there. The only light in his bedroom was coming from his clock. Its green numbers blinked 3:00. The hawk feather was lying in front of the clock, the eerie light turning it green. The house was quiet.

After his breathing returned to normal, Connor lay down again. Every time he closed his eyes, he felt the darkness spinning behind his eyelids. It was two hours before he fell asleep again.

Then he dreamed that he was sitting in Mr. Lowen's English class. Police officers swarmed into the classroom looking for someone. He started to sweat, wondering if they were looking for him.

Connor woke up with a jolt. He had slept through his alarm, and he had to rush to get ready for school. He was dead tired. The scrapes on his face were dry and dull red, and they hurt when he yawned.

He ate two granola bars on his bike on the way to school. He barely made it in time for the bell. Connor passed Troy Sellers in the hall on the way to first class. As usual, Troy and his buddies were walking like they owned the school.

"Hey, new guy! Smith!" Troy called. "What happened to your face?"

Connor shrugged.

"Did you get in a fight or what?"

Connor gave Troy a look that said "maybe I did, maybe I didn't." He sure wasn't going to tell Troy that he fell off his bike.

Connor kept walking. *Keep to yourself, show no weakness, and kids will leave you alone,* he thought. *Even if you're new. Especially if you're new.* He had been through it all before.

At lunchtime, Connor sat by himself in the cafeteria. He quickly scarfed down a couple of sandwiches and then went to the library. He found a table at the very back of the room, behind the tall shelves of books. He opened his biology book and set his watch for thirty minutes. Then he put his head down on his arms and fell asleep.

He didn't dream about anything.

Connor's watch alarm went off just before his first afternoon class. It took him a minute to remember where he was. He gathered his books and went downstairs to the biology lab.

Ashling was in his biology class. Connor saw her as soon as he walked into the classroom. The dark-haired girl sitting next to her leaned over and whispered something. Ashling looked up at Connor and then quickly looked away. Her girlfriend started giggling.

Are they making fun of me? Connor felt stupid. Sometimes he couldn't stand girls. He *liked* them all right, but he didn't like the ones that giggled and dated stupid football players.

He had to walk past the girls to get to his seat.

"Hi," said Ashling's friend as he went by. She was looking right at him.

"Hey," Connor mumbled. He kept his eyes focused on the back wall.

The class dragged. Connor watched the clock above the blackboard. He drummed his fingers in time with the second hand as it ticked around in slow circles.

He moved into double time and thought about playing in a band. *If I live in the same city for a few years, then maybe I could find some guys to play with. A guitar player, a bass player, and a singer. We could practice at my house when Mom isn't home. Maybe we could even get some gigs and make some money.*

He decided to bike downtown after school and check out the music store. Bands sometimes posted ads there if they were looking for players. Maybe someone would be looking for a drummer.

When biology class finally ended, Connor waited for Ashling and her friend to leave the room before he got up. He took his time getting to his next class. It bugged him that Ashling had been laughing at him, and he wanted to avoid her. At least her friend wasn't in his English class, too.

He walked in the door to the English room just as the bell rang.

Ashling was already in her seat. She smiled at Connor as he walked to his desk. He ignored her and slid into the seat behind her.

Moments later, Mr. Lowen came into the room and closed the door. "Good afternoon, class!" he bellowed. "Please take out your creative writing homework from last night."

Connor sighed. He hadn't paid attention to the homework assignment yesterday. Now he wouldn't have anything to hand in.

"I want you to switch papers with a partner," the teacher continued. "Pair up with someone sitting in front or back of you. Read each other's papers and then discuss them."

Just as Connor was starting to feel relieved, Ashling turned around. "I guess we're partners," she said.

Connor looked up and down his row and saw that everyone else was paired up. He was stuck with Ashling. "I guess," he said, frowning. He didn't know what to say to her, especially after she and her friend had been laughing at him in biology.

Just then, there was a knock at the classroom door. Mr. Lowen opened it and spoke to someone briefly. Then he turned to the class and said, "Karl Renta, could you come here, please? There are some gentlemen here to see you."

Through the partly closed door, Connor spotted two police officers.

Karl got out of his seat and disappeared into the hallway. Mr. Lowen told the class to go ahead and work with their partners. Then he disappeared, too.

How weird is that? Connor wondered, remembering his dream from the night before. *Talk about a coincidence. Or am I going crazy?*

Forget about that, I'm definitely going to go crazy if I have to be partners with Ashling. I don't know what to say to her. I'm not good with girls. Plus I don't have my homework done. She'll think I'm a loser.

When he finally looked up at Ashling, she was staring at him. Her light green eyes made him think about the ocean and other places he'd probably never see. He couldn't seem to find his tongue.

Ashling looked down at the ground. "Look, if you don't want to be my partner," she said in a soft voice, "maybe we can switch with someone."

"No, that's okay. I mean, I was just thinking about something. A dream. It's crazy, but last night I had a dream about the police coming into this classroom."

Her eyebrows went up. "Weird," she said. Then she told him, "Hey, that's what my name means, you know. Ashling means 'dream' or 'vision.' It's Irish."

"Cool. I kind of wondered about that," Connor said. He was glad for the change of topic. "I've never heard the name 'Ashling' before. Actually, I thought your name was Ashley at first."

Ashling sighed. "Yeah, I get that all the time. And people always spell it wrong."

"That's a drag," Connor said. "Anyway, about being partners, I kind of got the impression that you didn't like me. I mean, in biology class, you and your friend—"

"Oh no!" Ashling's cheeks turned a deep shade of pink. "It's just that my friend thinks...you know." She lowered her voice to a whisper. "She thinks you're cute."

Connor just stared at Ashling.

"You can't tell her I told you," she said. "Please promise me you won't say anything."

"Okay." Connor shrugged.

"I had to tell you. I didn't want you to think, you know, that I don't like you." She paused for a second. "So, um, we can be friends, right?"

"Sure, if you want," Connor said.

"Okay." Ashling smiled. "So, should we talk about this assignment?"

"Actually, I didn't do the assignment," Connor admitted.

Ashling laughed. "I didn't either!"

Connor grinned at her. *Saved!* He looked around the classroom. Everyone was talking with a partner. Mr. Lowen and Karl hadn't come back yet.

"I'm not very good at creative writing," he told Ashling.

"Me neither," she replied. "I'm better at math and science. What are you good at?"

"I don't know," Connor said. "Music, I guess. Art."

"Cool. What kind of music do you like?"

"I listen to lots of different stuff," he said. "And I play drums."

"Really?" said Ashling. "You'd probably get along with my brother. He plays drums and guitar. He works at the music store downtown—Dave's Music."

"Oh yeah? I was thinking of going there after school," Connor said.

"Say hi to my brother if you see him. His name is Liam. I think he's working today."

"Okay, cool," Connor said. He looked at Ashling and didn't know what else to say. *Life isn't fair,* he thought. *This girl is totally beautiful, and she's going out with a total meathead.*

"So, um, what do you think of my friend?" Ashling asked him.

And she's trying to set me up with her stupid friend. Great, he thought. "I don't know," he said out loud.

"Do you have a girlfriend?" she asked. Her cheeks were turning pink again.

"No," Connor replied. "I mean, I just moved to this town a few weeks ago."

"I thought you might have a girlfriend in your old town or something."

"My mom and I have moved around a lot. I don't usually stay in one school long enough to make many friends or...whatever." *Good one, Smith,* he thought. *Announce that you have no friends. She'll think you're really cool, now.*

Ashling shifted uncomfortably in her seat. "Oh. That's too—"

"Forget about it," Connor said quickly.

The classroom door opened and Mr. Lowen came in. Karl was nowhere to be seen. "Okay, people!" the teacher said loudly. "Discussion time is over."

Connor slumped down in his seat and stared at Ashling's long hair. She was wearing it loose today, and it fell down her back like a soft scarf. The ends were almost long enough to brush the top of Connor's desk.

Mr. Lowen droned on about creative writing until the class ended. When the bell rang, Connor grabbed his books and stood up.

Ashling turned around before he could get away. "I hope you stay here long enough to make some friends," she said quietly.

"Whatever," Connor said, walking away. *Perfect. Now she feels sorry for me. Get me out of this place.* He didn't look back.

Troy Sellers was waiting in the hall, holding his football under one arm. Connor ignored him. He practically ran to his locker, wanting to get out of school so badly.

He rode his bike straight to Dave's Music shop. Just looking at all the drum sets would make him feel better, even though he couldn't afford any of them. Plus he wanted to check out the bulletin board for ads.

The store was practically empty when he arrived. A young guy was standing behind the counter, talking on a cell phone and writing something down. Connor wondered if he was Ashling's brother. A man with long gray hair was testing out an electric guitar. His amp was cranked and he was playing complicated riffs over and over.

Show off, Connor thought. He stood and read the ads posted by the front door.

Singer wanted. Beatles cover band.

Bass lessons. $30.00/half hour.

Used mic for sale. AKG. Good condition.

Room for rent, shared house—male or female non-smoker, vegetarian.

Nothing. He wandered over to the drums. His favorite was a huge set of black drums. A yellow price tag hung from one of the drums. *Yeah, right,* Connor thought as he read the price. *In my dreams.*

The man playing the electric guitar finally stopped and left the store. Connor sat down on the stool behind the drum set. He ran his finger around the shiny silver rims of the drums. He tested the pedal of the bass drum and heard a satisfying thump.

The young guy came over. He pulled a set of drumsticks from a bin marked DEMO STICKS and handed them to Connor. "Here, try these," he said.

Connor took the sticks. "Thanks, man." He tested a few of the drums lightly at first. Then he let it rip with a rhythm that he had been practicing at home.

The guy from the store was nodding. When Connor finished, the guy said, "Sounds really good."

Connor grinned. "Thanks." He stretched out his hand. "I'm Connor Smith."

The guy shook Connor's hand. "Liam Kerr. Good to meet you."

"I think your sister's in my English class at school," said Connor. "She told me you work here."

"Five shifts a week," Liam said, smiling. "I'm saving up for university."

Connor nodded. "I need to find a job myself. For after school. Do you know anyone who's hiring?"

"What kind of work?" Liam asked.

"Anything," said Connor. "Well, maybe not factory work. I did that last year and it really sucked."

"Have you ever worked retail?"

"Oh yeah. I've done cash at a hardware store and a grocery store. A couple of summers ago I worked at a music shop. They sold used CDs and vinyl and stuff."

"That's cool. Do you know much about instruments?" Liam asked.

"Some. Are you guys hiring here?" Connor asked calmly. What he really wanted to say was, *Working here would totally rock! Please, oh please, hire me!*

"We might be," said Liam. "There's a new guy right now, but I don't think he's going to last. You could leave a resumé. Then we'll have it on file if this other guy bails."

"Right on," said Connor. "I'll bring it in tomorrow." He turned to leave. Then he turned back to shake Liam's hand. "Thanks for the lead. I appreciate it."

"No problem," said Liam. He raised one hand in a wave, and Connor left the store.

Let me be lucky just this one time, he thought to himself as he unlocked his bike. *Please let me get that job.* It turned into a chant as he rode home. *Let me be lucky*, he thought with every turn of the pedals. *Let me be lucky. Let me be lucky.*

That night, Connor had the nightmare again. First he saw the hawk flying into the storm. Then there were no images, just the sensation of darkness and spinning. Endless spinning. The sound of people screaming.

He woke up in a cold sweat. His heart was pounding a rapid *thud thud thud* against his chest. It was two a.m. The hawk feather was still sitting in front of the clock. Connor picked it up and twirled it in his fingers.

He stared out his bedroom window. A full moon was shining, casting strange shadows on the floor of the room. A jagged crack in the corner of the window cut through the image of the moon.

Connor tried to get back to sleep. He tossed and turned, but he couldn't get the unknown terror of the nightmare out of his mind. *It's just a stupid dream,* he told himself. But it was dawn before he fell asleep again.

When Connor's alarm went off, he hit the snooze button at least six times. When he finally got up, his mom had already left for work. She had left a note on the kitchen table. *Good morning, honey. I'm working a double shift today, so I'll be home late tonight. There's leftover soup in the fridge for dinner.*

Yesterday's special, Connor thought. *At least she works at a decent restaurant this time, so the leftovers are okay.* He packed a lunch and got ready for the day.

At school, Connor yawned through his classes. *I have to get a good sleep tonight,* he thought. *The only thing worse than being at school all day is being really tired at school all day. Teachers always seem to know when you're not paying attention.*

Even if he wasn't tired, he would have had trouble concentrating today. His resumé was burning a hole in his backpack. He couldn't wait to drop it off at Dave's Music. *Please let me get a job there*, he prayed. *I'll never complain about my mom again. I'll keep my room clean. I'll give my spare change to homeless people.*

He spent the afternoon wishing he had toothpicks to hold his eyelids open. He drank a cola right before English class, hoping it would give him energy. He didn't want to look like a deadbeat when he showed up at the store to ask for a job.

Ashling turned around in her seat as soon as Connor sat down. "Hey," she said. "I heard you met my brother."

Connor nodded. "He said they might be hiring at the music store."

"Yeah," said Ashling. "Liam told me. It would be cool if you could work there, too. He says it's a great place to work."

"I'm going to drop off a resumé after this class," Connor told her.

Mr. Lowen came into the classroom. Ashling smiled at Connor and turned back in her seat with a flip of her long hair.

Connor closed his eyes. The sight of Ashling smiling at him would stay with him for a while. *Snap out of it, Smith*, he told himself. *There's no point in thinking about impossible things.*

Once again, he found it difficult to pay attention to the teacher. Mr. Lowen was still going on about creative writing. Today it was something about plot development. Connor quietly drummed his fingers on his knees. He thought about what he would say when he went to the music store.

At the end of the class, Connor joined the line of people filing out into the hallway. Ashling was walking ahead of him, and she stopped just outside the door. Troy was waiting for her as usual.

"Hey, good luck!" she called as Connor walked past. "I hope you get the job."

"Thanks," said Connor.

Troy scowled at him. Connor kept walking and didn't look back.

He biked straight to Dave's Music. When he walked into the store, no one was behind the counter.

Connor wandered around for a minute, looking at everything. A sign hanging next to the guitars on the far wall read "Don't even think about playing Stairway to Heaven." *Do people still want to play that song?* he wondered.

A few vintage guitars hung on the wall behind the counter. The price tags made his eyes widen. *If I got a job here, I wonder if they would let me test one out*, he thought. *When else would I get the chance to play a thirteen-thousand-dollar guitar?*

Connor stood by the cash register, wondering what to do. He didn't want to just leave his resumé sitting on the counter.

Then he heard voices coming from a small doorway behind the counter. A piece of cloth was tacked up across the door. *That must lead to a back room or something*, Connor thought. He was about to call "hello" when a young, scrawny guy walked out. His hair was shaggy and he was wearing a black Frank Zappa T-shirt.

"Hey, man, what can I do for you?" the guy said. He was wiggling a guitar pick between two of his nail-bitten fingers.

"Is the owner here?" Connor asked.

"Yeah," said the guy, staring blankly at Connor.

Connor waited. After a minute, he said, "Can I talk to him?" He tried not to look annoyed. *Duh*, he thought to himself. *Why else would I ask?*

"Yeah, sure. Just a sec." The guy turned to go into the back room again, but at that moment an older, bald man appeared.

"Oh, hey," said the young guy. "There's a guy here to see you." He shrugged one shoulder in Connor's direction.

"Can I help you?" the bald man asked. He was tall and heavily muscled. Connor could see a tattoo where his sleeve was pushed up.

"Are you Dave?" Connor asked him. He thought he heard a snicker from the young guy. *Jerk,* Connor thought.

The man smiled. "Well, I'm the owner, but my name is Sanjay."

"Oh," said Connor. *Good start, Smith,* he thought to himself. *Way to make an impression.*

Sanjay leaned on the counter. "No worries. A lot of people make that mistake. The last owner's name was Dave. I never bothered changing the name of the store."

"Oh," said Connor again. "I just wanted to drop off a resumé. Just in case you're hiring any time soon."

He decided not to mention Liam's comment that one of the other employees might not last too long, just in case that employee happened to be in the room at the moment. He glanced over at the other guy, who was flipping through a copy of *Rolling Stone* magazine.

Sanjay nodded. "Sure. I'll keep it on file." He tossed the resumé on a pile of papers beside the cash register.

Connor felt a little disappointed, but he didn't know what else to do. *He didn't even look at it!* He took a deep breath and decided to introduce himself. *At least then he might remember my name.*

"I'm Connor Smith." He extended his hand toward Sanjay.

Sanjay shook it. "Nice to meet you, Connor. Have you ever worked at a music store before?"

"Yeah. I mean, I worked at a CD store," Connor said. He heard a snort from the young guy. "But I can do cash, no problem," he continued, ignoring the jerk. "I know a bit about instruments. Drums, anyway. And I learn fast."

Sanjay picked up Connor's resumé again and quickly scanned it.

"I can work any evening or weekend, whatever you need," Connor added. "I'd work days, too, but I have to go to school."

Sanjay laughed. "All right, Connor, I'll keep it in mind."

The phone started ringing. "Thanks," said Connor, turning to leave.

The phone rang again. Sanjay shot a look at the young guy, who was still reading his magazine. Finally, Sanjay picked up the phone himself. "Dave's Music," Connor heard him say. "We're open until ten."

Connor left the store feeling pretty good.

That good feeling lasted until midnight, when he woke up sweating from another nightmare. It was the same bad dream all over again. He couldn't see what was happening, but he could feel it. *Danger. Spinning. Terror.*

Chapter Three

Connor had the nightmare every night that week. By the time the weekend rolled around, he was exhausted. He slept in until noon on Saturday.

His grumbling stomach woke him up. If he hadn't been starving, he would have stayed in bed. Instead, he pulled on a sweatshirt and jeans and stumbled into the kitchen for something to eat.

His mom was sitting at the table with a mug of coffee. The phone book was open in front of her. She put it away when Connor came in. She took a close look at him as he sat down with a giant bowl of cereal.

"You look worn out, sweetheart," she said. "Did you have a tough week?"

"Yumph," Connor replied, his mouth full of cereal. In between bites he said, "I had a lot of homework and stuff." He wasn't ready to admit that bad dreams had been keeping him awake.

His mom frowned. She reached over and touched his cheek. "You've got shadows under your eyes."

"I'm okay, Mom. Don't worry. I just need to catch up on my sleep."

She didn't look convinced.

Connor changed the subject. "I've been looking for a job, too. There's a music store downtown that may be hiring."

His mom nodded. "Did you try the grocery store on York Street? I think I saw a help wanted sign in the window."

"No," Connor replied. "I can drop off a resumé there today."

His mom got up and poured herself another cup of coffee.

"Hey, Mom?" Connor said. "I was thinking. Do you think we could stay in this town for a couple of years? Just until I'm finished high school."

He started talking quickly so that he could get all his arguments in before she said no. "Once I get a job, I can give you money for rent and stuff. I think it would be good for me and school, you know." *Not to mention the fact that I can torture myself by daydreaming about Ashling for a couple more years.*

"We'll see, sweetheart," his mom said. She sighed. "I wasn't sure about moving back here, you know. I need to see how it works out before I make any promises."

Connor stared at the floor.

"I'll try, Connor. That's the best I can do right now," she told him.

Connor looked his mom in the eye. "Okay," he said. Then he got up and went to his bedroom to lift weights. Halfway through his workout, the phone rang. His mom knocked on his door to say it was for him.

Who would be calling me? Connor wondered. *No one has my number. Unless...* He crossed his fingers and hoped it was Sanjay from the music store. He took the portable phone from his mom and closed his door. He picked up the hawk feather for luck.

"Hello?" he said into the phone, flopping down on his mattress. He traced a pattern on the sheet with the feather.

"Hi, Connor?" It wasn't Sanjay. Far from it. It was a girl.

"Yeah," he replied. *What girl would be calling me?*

"It's Ashling...from school."

"Hey," Connor said. He felt his brain start to go foggy. *Ashling? Why would she...?*

What should I...? He took a deep breath and waited for her to say something.

"I just called to see how your English assignment was going. You know the other day, when we both said we didn't like creative writing. So I...um...wondered how you were doing on it."

Connor smacked one hand on his forehead. "Oh, no! I totally forgot about it. I haven't even started."

Mr. Lowen had told them to write a short story about whatever they wanted. Connor thought it would be hard enough to write a story, let alone pick the topic, too. Why couldn't Mr. Lowen have said "write about something that happened to you last summer" or something like that? But no. They could write about *anything*. And the assignment was due on Monday.

"I started mine," Ashling said. "But I hate what I wrote. I think I might start over."

"What's yours about?" Connor asked.

"I can't tell you. I'm too embarrassed," she said.

"Oh, come on, tell me," Connor said, teasing her. He forgot to be nervous about talking to Ashling.

"Okay, don't laugh," she said. "It's about a girl who discovers that her science teacher is inventing this chemical that will let him control the minds of everyone in the school. Then he can use all the people as guinea pigs for his scientific experiments. So the girl has to figure out his evil plot, save all the students, and bring the teacher to justice."

Connor smiled to himself. "That sounds okay to me," he said. "Mr. Lowen said it could be about anything."

"Yeah, well, I don't know," Ashling said.

"It's better than what I have," Connor said. "Which is nothing."

"I guess," she said, laughing. "Anyway, my grandparents and all my cousins are going to be here tomorrow, so I don't think I'll have time to start over."

Connor wondered what it would be like to have a big family. It sounded fun, to have all those people around. People that liked you no matter what. *I should just consider myself lucky. If I had cousins and stuff, they would interrupt me getting my homework done.* He closed his eyes. *Who am I kidding?*

There was silence on the phone. Connor didn't know what to say. It seemed like Ashling didn't know, either.

"Hey, how did you get my phone number?" Connor finally asked.

"Oh, um, I was at the music store with my brother this morning. I saw your resumé on the counter."

"Oh," said Connor. Ashling must have read his whole resumé. He wondered if there was anything on it that would make him seem like a loser.

"I hope you don't mind," she said.

"It's okay," Connor replied.

"You weren't joking when you said you've moved around a lot," Ashling said. "You've had jobs in, like, ten different towns."

Does she see that as a good thing or a loser thing? Connor wondered. "Well, variety is the spice of life," he said. Then he winced. *That was a cool thing to say. Not.*

"Well, I guess I'm in trouble then," Ashling said. "I've lived in the same town since I was born. The same house even!"

"You're lucky," Connor said, trying not to feel jealous.

"Well, the grass is always greener," Ashling said. "Anyway, I should go. I guess I'll see you on Monday."

"Yeah, see you," Connor said.

"Good luck with your story," she added.

"You too," Connor replied. He hung up and finished his weights. He felt kind of warm all over, and it wasn't just from working out. *Forget about Ashling,* he told himself. *She's just being nice to you. She's one of those girls who is nice to everyone. She doesn't think you're special.*

But he couldn't help wishing she did.

Connor spent the afternoon biking around town, dropping off resumés. On his way home, he stopped at the crossroads on the edge of town and stared down the country road. "I don't want you riding out there," he remembered his mom saying. "It's not safe."

The dirt and gravel road didn't look particularly dangerous. *What could be not safe about it?* Connor wondered. *I won't stop and talk to anyone. I won't get lost.*

It felt good to be outside. He didn't really want to go home right away. It had felt good to ride down that road with the wind in his face. He had felt free. Happy. Connor wanted to feel that way again.

He took off down the road. *I'll just go a little way along,* he thought. *Just to the first side road.* In less than five minutes, he saw the stop sign. His bike tires skidded on the gravel as he came to a stop. He put one foot on the ground and leaned his weight on it. His other foot rested on the bike pedal.

The road kept going straight as far as Connor could see. He looked to the right, down the side road that he had taken last time. River Road. He wondered if Biscuit the dog would be out.

Connor sighed and looked up at the sky. Out of the corner of his eye, he saw something on top of a nearby telephone pole. A hawk.

The bird seemed to be watching him. Connor wondered if it was the same hawk that he had seen the other day. *Do you have a nest somewhere around here? Are you the one that gave me your feather?* he asked silently. The bird didn't move.

Connor turned around and started biking home. He felt the bird's eyes on his back as he rode away.

After a moment, Connor stopped his bike and looked back. The hawk was still watching him. Then it spread its wings and flew off in the direction of Mr. Smith's farmhouse. Connor watched until the hawk disappeared behind the trees.

By the time he got home, his mom had left for work. Connor made a double box of macaroni and cheese. He sat on the concrete step outside the kitchen door and ate his dinner right out of the pot. The evening air was cool. The leaves on the maple tree in the front yard were starting to turn yellow.

He stared at the tree and tried to think of a story for his English assignment. No brilliant ideas came to him. He decided to go inside and play drums for a while. Sometimes he had good creative ideas while he was playing.

Connor put on a Phatstick CD and cranked the volume. Then he picked up his drumsticks, sat down on the stool, and started playing. He lost himself in the complex rhythms of the music.

Maybe my story could be about a guy who plays in a band. The band gets a record deal, and they get famous and go on a world tour. Connor shook his head. *No, that's dumb.*

It could be about a poor kid who wins the lottery. A million dollars. He shook his head again. *No, that's really dumb.*

The CD ended and Connor still didn't have a clue what he was going to write about. It was getting late. He practiced tossing his drumsticks up in the air and catching them again. On the third try, one hit the ceiling and bounced onto his bed.

He gave up and dove onto his mattress. The hawk feather was still sitting on his pillow, where he had left it earlier. He picked it up and thought about Ashling. She had a soft voice and a nice laugh. Connor fell asleep with the feather in his hand and Ashling on his mind.

The dream came again. Connor was standing in a field. He was watching the hawk, its strong wings beating under the black clouds of a thunderstorm. Lightning flashed. The hawk slowly circled down out of the sky. Everything started to spin.

Lightning flashed again. In that instant, the hawk swooped down. It seemed to grow bigger and bigger until finally it filled Connor's vision. He closed his eyes. When he opened them again, he saw an old, powerful-looking man standing beside him. The man's face was shadowed.

Connor reached out, but his hands only touched air.

He opened his eyes. Blinking, he saw that he was in his bedroom. It was one o'clock in the morning. The light beside his bed was still on, and he was still wearing his clothes. This time, he felt calm somehow. The other dreams had been scary, filled with a sense of danger. This one was different. The old man changed things. He seemed wise. And safe.

Connor fell back to sleep right away. The old man appeared again with the hawk on his arm. He was saying something, but Connor couldn't hear him. He still couldn't see the man's face.

When Connor woke up on Sunday, he felt rested for the first time all week. The afternoon sun was blazing through the window. His clock read 1:00. *No wonder I feel rested*, he thought.

He got dressed and went to the kitchen. His mom was sitting at the kitchen table, with the phone book open in front of her. She was holding the cordless phone, but she wasn't talking to anyone.

Connor watched her for a minute. Then he walked into the kitchen. "Who are you calling, Mom?" he asked.

She jumped. "Oh, nothing. No one," she said, quickly closing the phone book. She stood up and ruffled his hair. "I was thinking of making pancakes for breakfast. What do you think?"

"Pancakes work for me," Connor replied. "Although technically I think it's more like lunch time."

"You seemed so tired yesterday, I didn't want to wake you up." His mom took a box of pancake mix out of the cupboard.

"Thanks, Mom. I feel a lot better today." Connor took some orange juice out of the fridge. He watched his mom mix things in a bowl. "Do you want me to do anything?"

"You can do the dishes after, okay?"

"Sure," Connor said, sitting down. He tipped his chair back until his shoulders pressed against the wall. Then he hooked his feet around the chair legs. "Are you working today?" he asked his mom.

"No, I have the day off. If you want, Connor, you could help me unpack the boxes in the living room."

His chair dropped to the floor with a *thunk*. "Does this mean we're staying here for a while?" he asked.

"Don't push me," warned his mom. She poured pancake batter into the frying pan on the stove.

"Okay." Connor's face broke into a big grin. "We'll just unpack some boxes. It won't mean anything."

Right after breakfast, Connor went to the living room and started opening boxes. His mom came in and started to help. Then she decided that the furniture needed to be moved around first.

They moved the couch and the TV. It took three tries to find the perfect place for them. Connor found a wood block to put under the missing leg of the couch. Then his mom had to vacuum the rug. After that, they carried up a small bookshelf from the basement. Finally, they tackled the boxes.

Connor unpacked two boxes of books. Most of them were mysteries, which were his mom's favorite. He lined them up neatly on the bookshelf.

"Oh, here are my oven mitts. I've been looking for these." His mom held up a pair of blue striped oven mitts. "How did they get into this box?" She was unpacking a box of framed photos and tiny knickknacks. She had a collection of ceramic dogs and puppies.

Connor had always wanted a dog. His mom told him that her ceramic dogs were the closest he was going to get. They moved around too much to have a pet.

By dinnertime, the living room looked like a proper, lived-in room. "Will you be okay by yourself tonight?" his mom asked. "I'm going out with Gina."

"I'll be fine. I have homework," Connor said. "And dishes."

"Don't spend all night playing your drums, then," she warned him.

Connor rolled his eyes. "Yes, Mom."

She tossed a dishtowel at him and went to get ready.

After his mom had left the house, Connor sat down at the kitchen table with a pad of paper and a pen. He stared at the blank page and wished he could call Ashling. He didn't have the nerve—or her number.

"Write about what you know," Mr. Lowen had said. *That's great advice,* thought Connor. *So I should write about my own life. How boring would that be?* He drummed his fingers impatiently on the table.

After about half an hour, he started wandering around the house. *Write about what I know,* he thought. *Write about what I know.* He stood in his bedroom and looked around. *What the heck do I know?*

The hawk feather was sitting by his bed. Connor picked it up and carried it out to the kitchen. Sitting back down at the table, he tapped the feather against the blank paper. Then he started doodling. Dark clouds, lightning, and a hawk appeared on the page.

All of a sudden, Connor knew what to write about.

Chapter Four

Connor handed in his story at the beginning of English class on Monday. Mr. Lowen was standing at the classroom door, collecting papers as students walked in. Ashling was already in her seat.

"Did you finish your story?" she asked as Connor sat down behind her.

"Uh huh," he replied. "How about you?"

She nodded. "I think it's terrible, but I finished it!"

"Did you stick with the evil teacher plot?" Connor asked, smiling.

"Yeah. What about you? What's your story about?"

"It's sort of about this dream I had," Connor replied. "I mean, I didn't know what to write about. By last night I was kind of desperate. I've been having this recurring dream—nightmare—lately. So I turned it into a story."

"That sounds cool," Ashling said. "So what's the—"

"Okay, people!" Mr. Lowen said loudly. "Settle down! Let's get started."

Ashling rolled her eyes and turned around in her seat.

The class flew by. Connor drummed on his knees and thought about biking out in the country. He thought about the hawk and the old man, and about his strange dreams.

When the bell rang, Connor grabbed his books and headed for the door.

"Connor, wait!" Ashling called.

He turned around.

Ashling quickly caught up to him. "What are you doing now?" she asked.

He shrugged. "Going home, I guess."

"I want to hear about your story," she said. Her cheeks turned a little pink. "Do you want to, um, go to La Soda's or something?"

La Soda's was a little restaurant near the school. A lot of kids went there after classes or during a spare. Connor biked past the place every day on his way home. He had never gone inside.

"Where's your boyfriend?" he asked.

Ashling rolled her eyes. "Oh, he's getting his precious car fixed."

"Well," Connor told her, "even if Troy isn't here, he'll find out if you and I go to La Soda's. And trust me, he won't be happy about it. So let's just forget it." He started walking down the hall.

Ashling caught up to him at his locker. "Well, we could just walk. I have to walk home…why don't you come with me part of the way?"

Connor threw his backpack over his shoulder and slammed his locker shut in frustration. He looked at Ashling. Troy would still find out—Connor knew that—but he couldn't bring himself to say no.

They walked outside and Connor stopped to unlock his bike. "Where do you live?" he asked Ashling.

"Just on the other side of downtown," she replied.

They started walking across the parking lot. Connor pushed his bike along with one hand. Before they reached the street, another girl ran up to them. It was Ashling's friend from biology class. The one who supposedly liked him. *A setup,* Connor thought to himself. *I should have known.*

"Hey, Ashling," the girl said. She gave Ashling a little hug.

"Hi, Reesa. Connor, you know Reesa from biology class, right?"

"Sure," Connor said.

"Hey," said Reesa. She looked up at him through her eyelashes. Connor could see big clumps of mascara on them.

He quickly looked away. Reesa was gorgeous, in a way, but she had on too much makeup for Connor's taste. You couldn't see her real face.

"Are you guys going to La Soda's?" Reesa asked.

"No, um, I'm just going home," Ashling said. She looked at Connor.

"I have to go downtown," Connor lied. In case it got back to Troy, it might seem like a coincidence that he and Ashling were both walking in the same direction.

"Cool, I have to walk that way too," Reesa said. She trotted along beside Connor's mountain bike.

Great, thought Connor. *Just great.*

"So, where do you live, Connor?" Reesa asked him.

"Linden Lane," he said. Everyone knew that was in a bad part of town.

Reesa frowned. "Oh."

Connor looked over to see Ashling's reaction. She was just looking straight ahead. She didn't look disgusted or anything. Connor was relieved, although he wished he didn't care what Ashling thought of him.

Just then, Ashling looked over at Connor and smiled.

Connor looked away.

"Have you guys studied for the biology test on Friday?" Reesa asked. She sounded like a bird chirping.

"No," Connor said.

"I'm going to start tonight," Ashling said.

"Hey, maybe we could study together," Reesa suggested. She said it to Ashling, but Connor knew she was asking him, too.

"Sure," said Ashling.

Connor didn't say anything. He looked down at the cracks in the pavement as he walked. He watched Ashling when he thought she wasn't looking.

"Are you guys looking forward to the dance?" Reesa asked.

Connor vaguely remembered seeing posters for a dance on the bulletin board at school. It was in a few weeks.

"Yeah, it will be fun," Ashling said, looking at Connor. "Are you going to go?"

"I don't know," he said. "Maybe."

"You should come," Reesa said. "We could all go together."

Yeah, that's my idea of a good time, thought Connor. *Not. A double date with someone I don't like. And where I can watch the girl I do like with her idiot boyfriend.*

"I'm not really big on dances," Connor said. No way was he going to commit himself to that plan.

Reesa looked disappointed, but she didn't say anything. The three of them kept walking along the sidewalk. A group of kids from school were walking on the other side of the street. A guy on a motorcycle roared past. Connor thought it looked like Karl Renta, but he wasn't sure. Karl hadn't been at school since the police showed up last week.

Soon, they came to a side street lined with huge maple trees. Ashling and Reesa stopped walking.

"This is my street," Reesa announced. She waited for a moment, looking at Connor and then at Ashling. Her eyes narrowed. "I guess I'll see you guys at school."

Connor looked away. *Can she tell that I like Ashling? I just said I was going downtown. That's not giving anything away, is it?*

"I'll call you later," said Ashling.

"You do that, girlfriend," Reesa said with an icy smile. "Bye, Connor."

"Bye," Connor said.

He and Ashling started walking again. Neither of them said anything for a few minutes. Then they both spoke at once.

"Sorry about that—" said Ashling.

"I really don't—" said Connor.

Ashling laughed. "You go first."

"No, you go," said Connor. He was annoyed with Ashling for trying to set him up with Reesa, but he couldn't help smiling at her.

"All right," said Ashling. "I just wanted to say that Reesa's really nice."

"Whatever," said Connor. "I'm not really looking for a girlfriend."

"Oh," said Ashling.

Was it his imagination or did Ashling look relieved? "If I *was* looking for a girlfriend," Connor added gently, "I wouldn't need your help."

Ashling's face turned pink. "Okay."

Connor felt a little embarrassed himself. He went back to watching the pavement. *How did I get myself into this conversation?*

"You should come to the dance, though," Ashling said.

He looked up at her. *Does she want me to come? Or is she just saying that to be nice? Or does she still think I might go for Reesa?*

"I might go," he said.

"Hey, do you want to stop by Dave's Music?" Ashling asked. "Liam is working there today."

"Sure," Connor replied. He wouldn't say no to hanging out with Ashling for a little longer. *I just hope that jerk isn't there,* he thought. *Or Sanjay. I don't want to look like I'm pestering him for a job.*

It didn't take them long to get to the music store. Ashling waited for Connor to lock up his bike, and then they went inside.

"Hey, Liam!" Ashling called. Her brother was behind the counter. There was no sign of Sanjay or the jerk.

Connor followed slowly behind Ashling. He stopped to pick up a crumpled candy bar wrapper that someone had carelessly tossed on the floor.

When he looked back at the counter, Sanjay was standing there. He must have come from the back room. *Oh, great,* thought Connor, mentally kicking himself. *He caught me picking garbage off his floor.*

Since he couldn't do anything about it now, Connor nodded hello. "Do you have a garbage can back there?" he asked.

Sanjay gave Connor a funny look and reached down behind the counter. He held out a garbage can. Connor threw the candy wrapper in it.

"Hi, guys," Liam said to Ashling and Connor. "What's up?"

"Not much," said Connor.

"We came by to say hi," said Ashling. "We just had English class."

"I'm glad you stopped in," Sanjay said. "Are you still looking for a job, Connor?"

"Yeah," Connor said, surprised.

"I need someone two nights a week and one day on the weekend," he said.

"I can do that. No problem."

"Minimum wage to start," Sanjay said. "You'll be working with me or Liam on your shifts. You can start right away and learn as you go."

"Sounds good," said Connor, grinning.

Sanjay held up the garbage can. "I need someone who sees what needs to be done and does it without being told. You've already proven yourself in that department. You can learn everything else."

Connor restrained himself from jumping up, punching his fists in the air, and yelling *Yes! Yes! Yes!* Instead, he asked calmly, "What night do you want me to start?"

"Friday," said Sanjay. "How does five o'clock to ten sound?"

"I'll be here," Connor said. He reached over to shake Sanjay's hand. "Thanks."

Ashling gave Connor a huge smile. "Congratulations!" she said.

"Thanks. Anyway, I should head home. I'll see you at school tomorrow, Ashling."

"Yeah," she said. "Hey, wait! I never got to hear about your story."

"Some other time, I guess," Connor said. *Who cares about homework at a time like this?* he couldn't help thinking.

"I really want to hear about it," Ashling insisted. "Let's go. You can walk me to the end of the street and tell me on the way."

They said good-bye to Sanjay and Liam. Connor couldn't stop smiling as he unlocked his bike.

"I'm really glad you got the job," Ashling said. "I know you'll like working there. Liam says that Sanjay is a good boss."

"I can't wait to start," said Connor. He started pushing his bike down the sidewalk.

Ashling fell into step beside him. "Okay, so tell me about your story," she said. "No more interruptions."

"I hope you're not expecting some award-winning story," Connor said. "It's really not that exciting."

"Quit stalling," Ashling teased. "You said it was about your dream or something."

Connor shrugged. "All right. Last week, I was biking out in the country and I saw a hawk and met some old farmer guy." He left out the embarrassing part about falling off his bike. "Anyway, I found this hawk feather. After that I started having these…dreams… about a hawk and some other weird stuff. About the hawk turning into a man."

Ashling nodded.

Connor continued. "So, this weekend, I couldn't think of an idea for my English story. But then I saw the hawk feather and I decided to write about the old man I met. I made him into a sorcerer who can turn into a hawk. In my story, he flies around and sees stuff that other people don't see. Kind of like magic. He goes around and helps people."

"So, he's a good sorcerer," Ashling said.

"Yeah," Connor replied. He shook his head. "It's dumb."

"No!" said Ashling. "It sounds good. Sort of science fiction or fantasy, or whatever. He's like Gandalf in *The Lord of the Rings*."

"I guess," said Connor. They reached the end of the street and stopped walking.

"I live that way," Connor said, pointing to the right.

"This is where we go our separate ways, then," Ashling said. She pointed to the left. "I live that way."

Connor hopped on his bike. "I'll see you tomorrow."

"Yeah," said Ashling. She touched his arm lightly. "See you tomorrow."

Connor didn't move. "Bye, Ashling," he said. He waited until she had turned and walked away. Then he started pedaling in the other direction.

He could still feel his arm where she had touched him. Being friends with Ashling was going to be torture.

Connor biked home at top speed. It was lucky that they had stopped in at Dave's Music. This was going to be the best job he'd ever had. *Maybe I could even get a discount on a drum set*, he thought suddenly. His knees felt a little weak at the idea. *Okay, Smith, don't jinx yourself by getting greedy. Just be grateful you got the job.* He was definitely grateful. His luck had turned. He chanted *thank you, thank you, thank you* all the way home.

Unfortunately, Connor's good luck didn't stretch quite as far as he wanted it to. That night, he had the nightmare again. He dreamed of the hawk, the storm, and the spinning and screaming. The dream ended with the hawk. It turned into the old man, who was trying to give him a message.

This time, Connor could see his face. It was old Mr. Smith from out in the country. *Great, my dreams are starting to take notes from my English assignments*, Connor thought sleepily. But somehow it felt good seeing the old man again, with his twinkly blue eyes. The nightmare seemed less terrifying. It felt like Mr. Smith was protecting him somehow.

The next day at school, Connor looked for Ashling. He didn't see her until biology class.

Reesa was there, too. For once, the two girls weren't sitting together. Connor sat near the back of the room and practiced drum rhythms.

Halfway through the class, he saw Reesa pass a note to Ashling. Connor watched as Ashling opened the piece of paper and read it. She quickly crumpled up the note. Ashling didn't look at Reesa; she just looked straight ahead at the teacher. When the bell rang, Ashling got up and ran out of the class.

What was that about? Connor wondered. Then he saw Reesa walking toward him.

"Hey," she said, sitting on the edge of his desk. "Ashling has a boyfriend, you know."

"Yeah," said Connor. "I know. So what?"

"So, you'd better watch yourself, that's all," she said.

Connor stared at Reesa coldly. "What's your point?" he asked.

Reesa shrugged. "If you're looking for a girlfriend, don't look there."

"I'm not looking for a girlfriend," he told her.

"Could have fooled me," she said.

"Whatever." Connor stood up to leave. Reesa stood up, too. She was blocking his way.

"Ashling isn't available," Reesa repeated. She reached around Connor and tucked a piece of paper into the back pocket of his jeans. "That's my number in case you change your mind about the girlfriend thing." Then she turned around and walked out of the room, swinging her hips.

Connor shook his head. *Girls,* he thought to himself. *Whatever.*

He was almost late for English class. Ashling gave him a brief smile as he walked past her desk, and then she quickly bent her head so that her hair fell over her face. She didn't turn around to talk.

Connor didn't think she seemed very happy. He tried not to care. But the image of her troubled smile kept popping into his mind. *Did she have a fight with Reesa or something?* he wondered. He thought about it all through class. He wanted to ask her if everything was all right.

As soon as the bell rang, Ashling stood up to leave. Connor stood up and reached out to touch her shoulder, but he pulled back at the last second. "Hey," he said instead. "What's wrong?"

Ashling turned around and gave him a half-smile. "I'm okay, I'm just having a bad day. I'll talk to you later." She started walking toward the door. By now, there was a bottleneck of students trying to get out of the classroom.

Connor had a sudden thought. *Reesa seemed to think it was really obvious that I like*

Ashling. What if she told Ashling? Maybe that's what that note in biology class was about. Is that why Ashling is trying to get away from me right now? Maybe she thinks that I like her that way and she's trying to get as far away as possible.

He felt a chill run through him. He never expected Ashling to be his girlfriend. That was just a stupid wish he couldn't control. But he *was* getting used to the idea that she might want to be his friend. *I like the way she smiles and how she was happy that I got the job. Plus I like having someone to talk to.* Connor didn't want to screw that up.

He ran to catch up with her before he lost his nerve. "Ashling!" he said. "Wait up!"

She stopped and watched as he walked up to her. The last few students were leaving the classroom.

Connor started talking. "Listen," he said. "I don't know what Reesa said to you, but she talked to me after biology."

Ashling's eyes opened wide, and then she looked at the floor. "I can't talk about this right now," she said, almost in a whisper. She started walking again.

Connor caught up to her again and they moved into the hallway side by side. "I just wanted to tell you that I want to be your friend," Connor said. "That's it. That's all. I hope we can be friends. I'm sorry if—"

"HEY!" a voice shouted.

Connor looked up to see Troy Sellers walking toward them. Fast. Connor planted his feet and prepared for the worst.

Troy stopped right in front of Connor. "Smith, or whatever your name is, I suggest you leave my girlfriend alone."

Connor looked over at Ashling. Her eyes were bright with tears and anger. "Troy," she said, "you—"

"This has nothing to do with you, Ashling. This is between me and the stud here." Troy didn't look away from Connor. "Don't make me repeat myself, Smith. Leave her alone."

Connor looked at Ashling again. She was completely focused on Troy.

"Fine," said Connor. "No problem."

He starting walking down the hall, cursing with every step. *I should have known better. Just stick to yourself, Smith. It's easier that way. You'll probably be leaving town in a year, anyway. What's the point in having friends?*

He biked home and played drums for hours. It felt good to make noise. Playing drums was a great way to smash things without actually breaking anything. Which is what Connor really wanted to do. Smash something. Preferably right over Troy Sellers' meaty head.

Of course, he wouldn't really do that. Connor might not have any friends, but he sure didn't want any enemies, either.

Chapter Five

For the rest of the week, Connor stayed away from Ashling and Reesa at school. He saw Troy a couple of times in the halls and kept his distance. Troy glared at him but didn't make any threatening moves.

Connor was having the nightmare every night. It wasn't as scary now that old Mr. Smith was in it, but it was still preventing Connor from getting enough sleep. By Friday, he was yawning through all his classes. He was worried about staying awake for his first shift at Dave's Music.

On Friday afternoon at the end of English class, Mr. Lowen handed back the story assignment. He strolled up and down the rows of desks and casually tossed assignments left and right. Connor's story landed upside down on his desk.

"Let me remind you all," Mr. Lowen said in a bored voice, "that when handing in assignments, it is a good idea to put your name on them." He waved a couple of papers in the air. "Who hasn't received their story?"

A few students raised their hands.

Let's get this over with, Connor thought. He flipped over his assignment. In the top right hand corner, written in red ink, was a large "A." Connor's eyes opened wide. *Pretty good for a last-minute job, Smith.*

He wondered how Ashling did on her story. He wanted to tap her on the shoulder and ask, but he didn't. They had barely spoken to each other for the past few days.

Just as Connor was thinking about that, Ashling turned around in her seat. "How did you do?" she whispered. "I got a 'B minus.'"

Connor showed her his mark.

"I thought you said you weren't good at creative writing," she whispered.

Connor shrugged. "I got lucky. If I hadn't thought of using my dream, I probably would have got an 'F' or something."

"Yeah, right," Ashling said. She gave him a tiny smile and turned around in her seat.

"All right, folks! Settle down," Mr. Lowen shouted. "If any of you want to discuss your marks, please talk to me after class. I'm going to pass out a short story that I want you to read for tomorrow's class." He handed out the homework just in time for the bell.

Connor stood up quickly. He needed to get home and eat dinner before work. It took him a few minutes to get outside to the bike rack. Ashling and Troy walked by while he was unlocking his bike.

Ashling looked back over her shoulder. "Hey, Connor!" she called. "Have fun on your first shift at work!"

He hopped onto his bike. "Thanks," he said. *She remembered.*

Troy gave him a dark look.

Connor started pedaling toward the street. He took a quick look back at the parking lot. Ashling and Troy were standing beside his car, facing each other. Troy was yelling and pointing his finger at Ashling. Ashling had her hands on her hips.

Connor kept riding. *Ashling's relationship is none of my business,* he thought. *I told her I want to be friends, but Troy is obviously against that idea. Ashling seems to be going along with it. Except for today, she has barely talked to me. So I guess I'll just forget about it. I'll just concentrate on music and my job. Oh yeah, and school.*

He biked home and found a note on the kitchen table. *Have a great shift, honey. See you tonight—I'll be home around ten. Hamburgers are in the fridge.*

After eating a quick dinner, Connor got ready for work. Just before he left the house, he remembered his English story. He put it on the kitchen table where his mom would see it. Connor knew she would like to see his good mark. He smiled to himself. The truth was, he wanted her to see it. *So I'm a little proud of my 'A.' So what?*

He arrived at work five minutes early. Sanjay was behind the counter. He gave Connor a tour of the store and told him some of the basics of the business.

Sanjay set him to work doing easy jobs such as sorting guitar picks. The picks were displayed in a big case on the counter. Each kind of pick had its own little cubbyhole in the case. Customers tended to mess them up. Connor also filled up the magazine rack and put a bunch of invoices in alphabetical order.

Connor didn't care what jobs Sanjay gave him. Just standing around all those instruments gave him a thrill. Another bonus was that Sanjay played good music on the stereo. *Forget that crappy muzak you hear in most stores,* Connor thought to himself.

All in all, it was a great shift. Connor was in heaven for five straight hours. This was definitely the best job he'd ever had. Sanjay closed the store at ten o'clock. Connor biked home with a huge smile on his face. He was completely tired, but in a good way.

The smile was still on Connor's face when he walked in the side door at home. Then he looked up and saw his mother. He quickly dropped his backpack and rushed into the kitchen.

She was sitting at the table. Her eyes were red and puffy, and it looked like she had been crying. A box of tissues and Connor's English story were sitting on the table in front of her.

"What's wrong, Mom?" he asked. He walked up to the table and waited anxiously for her to say something.

She looked straight at Connor. "Connor James Smith, I am *not* very happy with you right now." Her voice sounded rough and...angry.

What? Did I miss something here? Connor wondered. He opened his mouth to speak, but his mom interrupted him.

"You can consider yourself grounded for the rest of the month."

Connor's mouth dropped open. He had never felt so surprised in his life. *What did I do? Is she mad that I got an 'A'? I don't get it!*

"What the heck? Mom, what are you talking about?" he demanded.

"Connor, you specifically disobeyed me." She smacked her hand down on his story. "You are grounded and that's the end of it. No arguments."

Connor dropped down into a chair. He ignored the story. "Mom," he said, "you're not making any sense. I thought you'd be happy that I got an 'A.' Instead, you're telling me I'm grounded." He threw his hands up in the air. "Help me out here."

"Don't be flip with me," she said.

Connor leaned his elbows on the table and frowned at his mom. She wasn't making any sense. "Are you all right?" he asked. "Are you going through that thing, you know, that older women go through? The whatchamacallit thing that makes you act like you're crazy for a little while?"

His mother glared at him. "No, I am not going through menopause. Don't try to change the subject."

"Okay, Mom." Connor tried again. "Can you please just explain what the heck you're talking about? From the beginning?"

She sighed in frustration. "Connor, I specifically asked you not to go biking out in the country. Now I read your story and find out that you disobeyed me. Not only did you disobey me, but you've been talking with him. Who knows what crazy things he's told you!

I really wanted to take care of—"

"Mom," Connor interrupted. "You don't understand. I haven't been talking to anyone. This story isn't real. I had to write a story for English class. You know, creative writing. Fiction. Make believe. *I made it up*."

"Connor, I need you to stop lying to me. Right now."

Connor stared at his mother. *Is she losing it or what?* he wondered. "Mom, you have to listen to me. I only went biking out in the country that one time. Okay, maybe one other time after that, but that's it! You told me not to, so I didn't. I just needed to write a story for English. I've been having this weird dream about a hawk and an old man so I used it for my story."

His mom's eyes started to fill with tears. "I know you're probably upset with me. It's just that I wanted to fix things before you met him." She blew her nose.

Met who? Connor wondered. *Fix what things? Before when?*

"Now that isn't going to happen," his mom continued, waving a handful of tissues in the air. Her voice was getting higher and higher. "And I don't know what he's said to you. I don't even—"

"Mom." He tried to get her attention.

"And what if he doesn't—"

"Mom!" Connor said loudly.

She looked up at Connor and wiped the tears from her eyes.

"Who are you talking about?" he asked.

His mom pushed his English story across the table toward him. "I'm talking about your grandfather," she said.

Chapter Six

Silence filled the room. "Wh—what did you just say?" Connor finally asked.

"I said, I'm talking about your grandfather," his mom repeated.

He stared at her. "I have a grandfather?" Connor felt confused, excited, and angry—all at the same time. His mom had always said that his grandparents were dead. *So how can I all of a sudden have a grandfather?*

"Please don't play games with me, Connor. I'm too tired."

"I'm not playing games!" Connor said angrily. "What do you mean I have a grandfather?"

His mother stood up and put her hands on her hips. "I know you've been talking to him. It's all in your story. So please stop pretending that you don't know what I'm talking about."

Connor stood up, too. "I *don't* know what you're talking about!" He was practically shouting now. "I haven't been talking to anyone. I don't say anything about my grandfather in that story."

"Well, then how did you know about all that stuff?" his mom shouted back. "About the hawk and about Biscuit the dog for heaven's sake? Biscuit died when I was a little girl. Obviously your grandfather told you about that and who knows what else."

"All his dogs are named Biscuit," Connor started to explain. "Mr. Smith said—"

Mr. Smith.

Connor opened and closed his mouth a couple of times. "Mr. Smith from out in the country is *my grandfather*?"

His mom pressed her fingers against her temples. "I can't talk about this any more right now. I'm tired and upset, and you're making me nuts."

"*I'm* making *you* nuts?" Connor said.

His mother tightened the ties on her faded pink bathrobe. "I'm going to bed. We can start this conversation again in the morning." She left the kitchen without saying another word.

Connor heard her bedroom door slam.

He sank down into his chair. His mind was whirling. *I have a grandfather! Why didn't she tell me? My whole life I've had a grandfather, and she didn't tell me. I felt like a freak growing up without anybody except my mom. Now I find out it's not even true.* He felt like yelling and crying and…he didn't even know what else.

He went and got ready for bed, but he couldn't stop thinking about it. *Why didn't she tell me?* Connor flopped down on his mattress. He stared up at the ceiling for a long time before he fell asleep.

The dream began the same way—with the hawk flying against the black clouds of the storm. The powerful bird circled down out of the sky, its wings outstretched. Then the world started spinning. The screaming began somewhere in the distance. Terror started building in Connor's chest.

The hawk flew closer. In the blink of an eye, the bird shape-shifted into the old man. Sorcerer. Mr. Smith. A hawk sat on his arm, its golden eyes watching Connor.

Mr. Smith's blue eyes sparked and flashed. "Grandson," he said, reaching out with his free hand.

Connor tried to step forward, but his feet were anchored to the ground. It felt like he had stepped in wet concrete.

Without warning, the old man threw up his arm. The hawk took flight. "Watch the hawk, Connor," Mr. Smith said in a low voice. "She has a message for you."

Connor watched the bird as it made its way across the dark sky.

"What message?" He turned to ask the old man, but he was gone. Connor was left standing alone in a field. The grass was bright green and glistening with rain. All he heard was the sound of the wind and the hawk's keening cry.

When Connor opened his eyes, he was back in his bedroom. The sky outside the window was turning pink. He yawned and flung his arm across his eyes. *Stupid dream*, he thought. *I wish my grandfather—*

Suddenly, he sat straight up in bed. The events of last night came flooding back. The conversation with his mother. Fighting. Finding out about his grandfather.

I really have a grandfather! he thought. *It wasn't just a dream.*

He fell back against his pillow. The sound of dishes clinking and water running came from the kitchen. His mom was up already. It was Saturday. Connor didn't have to work at Dave's Music until later that day. He thought about biking out to see Mr. Smith. *Would he want to see me?* he wondered.

New questions jumped into his mind. *Does he even know about me? Why doesn't Mom ever talk to him or visit him? Did something terrible happen? Do I have a grandmother, too?* He felt angry about the whole thing, but then he felt guilty for feeling angry. He didn't know what to feel.

Even though it was still early, Connor rolled out of bed and pulled on his jeans and a sweatshirt. It was time for his mother to answer a few questions.

His mom was making coffee. She turned around when Connor walked into the kitchen. They stood there for a moment, silently watching each other. His mom hugged her arms across her chest.

Connor rubbed his eyes and then stuck his hands in his pockets. He leaned against the kitchen door frame.

"Do you want a cup of coffee?" she finally asked.

"Sure," Connor replied. He didn't drink coffee, but somehow it felt like the right thing to say.

His mom turned around and got two mugs out of the cupboard. She put a bowl of sugar on the table. "Can you get the cream out of the fridge?" she asked.

Connor walked over and opened the fridge door. The floor was cold under his bare feet. He found the little carton of cream and put it on the table. He sat down cross-legged on a chair so that his feet wouldn't have to touch the floor.

His mom put a mug of steaming coffee in front of him. Then she sat down across from him. "Did you sleep okay?" she asked, pouring cream into her coffee and stirring it with a spoon.

"Not bad," Connor said. Since he never drank coffee, he wasn't sure if he should add cream or sugar. He took a small sip of the black stuff. *Blaaaghh! How do people drink this stuff?* He added sugar and cream to his mug.

"Did you sleep okay?" he asked politely.

His mom sighed. "Not really."

Connor took another sip of coffee. *Hmmm, not completely horrible.* He added more cream and sugar and tried again. *Much better.* He looked at his mom. She looked kind of sad, but she was holding it together.

"I'm sorry I was so upset with you last night," she said.

Connor shrugged.

"I was just so shocked when I read your story," she said. "This is a hard thing for me. There's so much you don't know…"

"Well, why don't you try telling me about it?" Connor suggested. The words came out louder than he intended.

His mom flinched. "I don't want to fight with you, Connor."

"I don't want to fight either, Mom," he said, quietly this time. "But you wouldn't even listen to my side of the story last night."

"I know, honey. Let's start again, okay?"

"Okay," Connor said. "I think I have a right to know what's going on."

She nodded. "First, I need to know what happened when you met him."

Connor told her what had happened the day he went biking out on River Road. He told her about the hawk and falling off his bike. He told her about meeting Biscuit the dog and old Mr. Smith. "I didn't know who he was, Mom," he told her. "I only knew his name because I saw it on his mailbox."

Then he told her about the nightmares. "I had to write a story for English class, and I couldn't think of anything to write about. I just used my dream as an idea for the story. I made up the part about Mr. Smith being the sorcerer. I mean, *obviously* that's not true. It's just a weird…coincidence…that he's my grandfather. I swear I didn't know." Connor sat back and waited for his mom to explain her side of the story.

"Yes, it's a very strange coincidence." She frowned and gave Connor a look that said "I don't believe you, but I can't prove it."

She took a sip of coffee and closed her eyes. "He always liked hawks." She paused, and then looked at Connor. "I never got along well with my father. We didn't see the world in the same way. My mom died when I was a teenager. After that, things with my dad got worse. We fought a lot. Then I met your dad, and my father was furious. He didn't want me to see him. He said I was too young. It was the worst fight we ever had."

"Of course, I was young. I was also a little rebellious," his mom continued. Her cheeks looked a little flushed. "I ran away from home. Your dad and I left town and lived in a run-down little apartment. When I think about that place…" She shuddered. "Anyway, my father was really angry. He said he wouldn't support us." Her eyes filled up with tears. Connor handed her a tissue.

"I told him I would never speak to him again," she said, blowing her nose. "He said that was fine with him. Then I got pregnant, and your dad walked out on me. I couldn't call my father because I thought he would just say 'I told you so.' That's if he even wanted to talk to me at all. So I just moved to a new town and tried to start over. I had you to look after, and that was the only good thing about my life." She smiled tearily at Connor. "I haven't talked to him since."

"You haven't talked to your dad since you left home? Not ever?"

"Not once," said his mom. "Heaven knows, I've thought about contacting him from time to time. But I was mad at him for so long, and then I was just afraid to call. I was afraid he wouldn't want to see me. I didn't want to be...rejected again."

"And he never called you?" Connor asked her.

She shook her head. "Well, I kept moving from place to place. And I always had an unlisted phone number. Sometimes I didn't even have a phone. It would have been pretty hard for him to track me down. I don't know. I doubt that he even tried."

"You don't know that," Connor said. "I'll bet he tried to find you."

She laughed. "You don't know my dad."

"No, I don't," Connor said angrily. "Thanks to you."

His mom didn't say anything. She just reached for the box of tissues.

"Sorry, Mom," he said. He'd never get the whole story out of her if he kept making her cry. "It just feels weird that I have a grandfather who I didn't know about. And he doesn't even know about me."

His mom nodded. "I know," she said. "I'm sorry."

Connor got up and started making toast. "So, does this mean you grew up around here?" he asked.

"Yes," she replied. "Out at the farm you saw on River Road."

"Why did you decide to move back, then?" he asked.

"Gina offered me a job at her restaurant. I thought about coming back here, and about Dad. I thought it might be time to confront my past and...I don't know...tell him I'm not angry anymore. I don't know if he'd even care, but I'd feel better if I tried to make peace with him. It's been weighing on me for a long time." She gave a short laugh. "For about sixteen years, I guess."

She stood up and poured herself another cup of coffee. "Do you want more coffee?"

Connor shook his head.

His mom leaned against the counter. "I'd like to tell him about you, too. That's one of the reasons I was so upset about your story. I wanted to sort things out with my dad before I told you about him. Before you two met. I've picked up the phone to call him a hundred times since we moved here. I haven't been able to do it."

"Well, you'd better do it soon," Connor told her. "I want to go out and meet him. For real, this time."

"I'll try, honey." She frowned. "But please wait until I talk to him before you go out there."

She walked over and put one hand on his shoulder. "I know you probably think I'm a terrible mother. I'm sorry I didn't tell you about him, but I just couldn't." She looked like she was going to cry again.

"You're not a terrible mother," Connor said quickly. "I just want to meet my grandfather. I mean, maybe he'll be a jerk to me, too. Maybe I won't like him."

Or maybe he won't like me, Connor thought to himself.

His uncertain thoughts about his grandfather stayed in his mind until he went to work later that day. When he got to Dave's Music, it was easier to forget about the crazy parts of his life and focus on the good stuff, like having a good job. Like playing music.

His second shift at work was even better than his first. He got to work with Liam this time.

Ashling's brother is a good guy, Connor thought. When there weren't any customers in the store, they talked about music. Liam liked all the same music that Connor did. He even offered to lend him a couple of CDs. They talked about playing, too. Liam played guitar and drums.

"There's a cafe down the street that has a jam every Saturday afternoon," Liam said. "If you ever want to play out, let me know."

"I don't know," said Connor. "I don't think I'm really ready to play in front of people. I'd rather find a few guys and practice in my basement."

"Well, you have to start somewhere," Liam said. "Lots of new guys show up for the jam, so you wouldn't be the only one. And you could meet the right people if you're looking to join a band."

"I guess," said Connor. "I'll have to think about it."

When customers came into the store, Liam helped them out. Connor watched and learned. Toward the end of the night, he rang in the sales with Liam watching.

"You seem to be getting the hang of it," Liam told him.

"Thanks," said Connor.

Just before they closed, a girl came in to buy some bass guitar strings. Connor noticed her checking Liam out. After she left, Connor asked about her.

"Talinda comes in here all the time," Liam said. "She's cool, but…I don't know. We went out a few times." He looked thoughtful. Then he shrugged his shoulders. "I don't understand girls."

Connor grinned. "Me neither."

He realized that he was still holding the receipt for Talinda's strings. He stuck it under the cash drawer with the other sales receipts.

"So, does Talinda play bass?" Connor asked Liam.

Liam nodded. "Yeah. Pretty cool, huh?"

"Yeah," Connor agreed. "You don't see many girl bass players."

"She's good," Liam said. "She's been out to some of the Saturday jams."

"Cool," Connor said.

"Ashling is pretty good, too," Liam said. "I mean, she doesn't play bass, but she plays acoustic guitar a bit. She sings, too."

Connor raised his eyebrows. "Really? She never said anything to me."

"Yeah, she's shy about it," Liam said. "She usually practices when no one's home. But I've caught her at it a bunch of times. I'm trying to convince her to play in front of other people. She just needs confidence."

"So, um, how is Ashling doing?" Connor tried to sound casual.

"She's all right," Liam said. "I thought you two were friends."

"Well, we talk in class and stuff, but..." Connor paused. "We're sort of friends, I guess, but she has a boyfriend. Troy isn't too cool with Ashling having a guy as a friend."

"Troy is a jerk," Liam said. "I can't stand the guy."

"Me neither," Connor agreed.

Liam looked at his watch. "Hey, it's time to lock up and get out of here."

Connor waited outside while Liam set the alarm. It was dark and the streetlights were on. "See you later," Liam said after locking the store.

"Take it easy," Connor said, hopping on his bike.

As he rode home, he thanked all the powers in the universe again for giving him this job. Sanjay was a good boss, Liam was fun to work with, and the store was awesome.

After a few minutes, he crossed the railway tracks. Before Connor turned down his own street, he stopped and looked down the country road.

My grandfather lives down there, he thought to himself. There were no streetlights on the dirt road, and the whole area was dark. A pale moon shone on the dark outlines of trees, but that was all that he could see.

I wonder if Mom called him today? Connor really wanted to visit Mr. Smith tomorrow, though he felt a little nervous about it, too. *He seemed like a nice old man, but what do I know? What if he doesn't want to have anything to do with us?*

Connor figured he had nothing to lose. *I didn't have a grandfather before. If he's not interested, then I still won't have one.* But he still felt a little bit of hope in the corner of his heart.

Suddenly he felt angry with his mom. *Why didn't she fix this a long time ago? Why didn't she tell me about my grandfather, even if he is a jerk? Why didn't she tell him about me?*

He felt mad at his grandfather, too. *Why did he have to be so mean to his only daughter? Wouldn't he feel bad about it by now? Wouldn't he try to get in touch with her? Wouldn't he wonder what happened to her?* He felt mad at himself. *Why do I care anyway? My grandfather hasn't been interested for sixteen years, he probably won't be interested now.*

Somehow, that made him feel worse.

By the time he got home, Connor was feeling more tired than angry. He walked into the kitchen. The phone book and a pile of crumpled tissues were lying on the table.

I guess she talked to him, Connor thought.

His mom was nowhere to be seen. Her bedroom door was shut and there was no light coming from the crack at the bottom. The house was silent.

In the bathroom, Connor saw damp towels on the floor. Melted candles sat on the edge of the tiny bathtub, next to his mom's bottle of smelly bath stuff.

She definitely talked to him, he thought. As far as Connor knew, his mom only took baths when she'd had a bad day.

He tiptoed past her bedroom door. Now he'd have to wait until morning to find out what had happened.

Chapter Seven

On Sunday morning, Connor found his mom sitting at the kitchen table. The phone book and tissues were gone.

"Morning," he said casually, getting himself some cereal.

"Good morning, honey," his mom said, standing up and walking over to Connor. She reached out and brushed something off his T-shirt. Then her hand dropped to her side. "I called your grandfather yesterday."

Connor put his bowl on the counter and turned to look at his mom. "Oh, yeah?"

She took a deep breath before she spoke. "It was one of the hardest things I've ever had to do," she told him. "I know I've been putting it off for a long time and I just want to say thanks for…for encouraging me." She pulled him into a motherly hug.

Connor let his mom hug him for a minute before he wriggled away. "You're welcome, I think," he said. He hesitated for a second. Then he asked, "How did it go?"

His mom opened her mouth and then closed it again. Then she half-nodded. "It was hard," she finally said. "But I did it. He was…it was…okay." Her eyes filled with tears, but she nodded confidently. "It's going to take some work, for both of us, but I think it's going to be okay."

Connor felt his muscles relax a little. He hadn't even realized he was tense. "Did you tell him about me?" he asked.

"Yes I did, and he's really looking forward to meeting you." Her face creased into a frown. "I told him that you had met him already, by accident, on your bike. He said he thought so." She crossed her arms and gave Connor a long, searching look. "So, I'm having a hard time believing your story about not knowing it was him."

Connor threw his hands up in frustration. "Why would I lie, Mom? I didn't know it was him that day. If I knew, I would have asked you about it right away."

"I don't want to fight about this again, Connor," she said. "We can settle it when we go out to see him this afternoon. That is, if you want to come with me."

"Oh, yeah," Connor said. "I'm coming." He could hardly believe that he was actually going to meet his grandfather. A grandfather who might want him after all.

After lunch, Connor put on his cleanest pair of jeans and a sweater. When his mom knocked on his door to tell him it was time to go, he saw that she had changed, too. She was wearing a long dress with little flowers on it.

They climbed into his mom's rusty green hatchback. His mom sat staring out the front windshield for a minute.

"Mom," Connor said, waving a hand in front of her face. "Let's go."

She turned and looked at him. "Sorry. I'm a bit nervous."

"Me too," Connor admitted. "Do you think he'll like me?"

His mom smiled. "Yeah, I do. It's me he has a problem with."

"Still?" Connor asked.

She started the car and backed onto the street. "We have some things to work out. But just remember, it has nothing to do with you. Okay, honey?"

"Okay," Connor said.

It didn't take long to drive out to River Road. His mom drove slowly, swerving now and then to avoid the potholes. When she turned into Mr. Smith's driveway, Connor sat up straight and watched for Biscuit the dog.

The car rolled to a stop behind an old pickup truck. Connor's mom turned off the engine and took a quick look in the rearview mirror. Connor waited while she checked her hair, her lipstick, and her teeth. Then she got out of the car and smoothed her dress.

"Ready?" she said to Connor.

Connor nodded, and they walked toward the farmhouse. It was a small house with faded yellow wood siding and a big front porch. Before they got there, the screen door swung open and Mr. Smith came out. He was still wearing his faded, blue plaid jacket. A bright red baseball cap rested high on his head. It looked new.

That will be my first job as his grandson, Connor thought. *To teach him how to wear a baseball cap properly.*

Connor's mom stopped walking. Mr. Smith walked closer, then stopped several feet away. Connor looked from his mother to his grandfather and back again. He felt a bit uncomfortable. The two of them were just staring at each other. No one spoke.

Connor heard a funny noise beside him. Then he realized it was his mom—she had let out a loud sob. And another one. She was pressing her hand on her mouth, like she was trying to hold them in.

Mr. Smith took another step toward them, then stopped again. His eyes were a dark, cloudy blue, and his face was more wrinkled than Connor remembered. It was like he didn't know what to do.

A little flap at the bottom of the farmhouse door swung open, and Biscuit came running out. She let out a bunch of little yaps and ran straight up to Connor. She licked his shoes and jumped up and down. Then she ran over to Connor's mom.

She bent down and scratched the dog's ears. "Hey, beautiful girl!" she said. Biscuit wriggled in delight. Connor's mom scooped up the small dog. She cradled Biscuit in one arm and rubbed the dog's belly. Biscuit tilted her head back and looked at Connor. Her tongue was hanging out and her eyes were glazed with pleasure.

"I used to have a dog just like you," Connor's mom said, looking down at Biscuit.

"Yep, this is Biscuit number three." Mr. Smith was standing right in front of them. "This is your dog's granddaughter."

Connor's mom looked up with tears in her eyes. "Hi, Dad," she whispered.

Mr. Smith nodded. "Jessica," he said. His voice was rough. He reached out and touched her shoulder. Connor's mom took a step toward him, even though she was still holding Biscuit. The old man's arms came up around her in an awkward hug.

Connor saw tears in his grandfather's eyes. His own eyes felt suspiciously damp, and he rubbed them with his sleeve.

After a minute, his mom stepped back and looked at Connor. "Dad," she said, "this is your grandson."

Mr. Smith turned and fixed his eyes on Connor. They were the piercing blue eyes of the sorcerer in Connor's dreams. He stuck out his hand. "I believe we've met."

Connor shook his grandfather's hand with his strongest grip. "I didn't know it was you that day."

"I didn't know, either," the old man said. He looked Connor up and down. "But I had a feeling about you."

"So, you didn't tell Connor…anything?" his mom said.

"No," Mr. Smith told her. "I just had a feeling in my gut." He patted his blue plaid jacket in the area of his stomach. Then he looked over and winked at Connor. His eyes suddenly looked friendly and warm.

"So," he said, rubbing his hands together. "Come on inside and I'll get you some iced tea." He started walking toward the house.

Connor's mom leaned over and whispered in his ear. "Is this okay?"

"Yeah, it's good," Connor whispered back to her.

They followed the old man into the house. Biscuit came with them, running circles around their feet as they walked.

In the kitchen, Connor's grandfather poured three tall glasses of iced tea. Connor spotted an old photo taped to the fridge. It showed a young couple with a little girl. *That must be Mom when she was young,* he thought.

Mr. Smith led them out to the porch. He sat in a big wooden chair. For a few minutes, he just looked at Connor's mom. "I tried to find you, Jessica," he said in a gruff voice.

"I knew it! I knew he did!" Connor shouted triumphantly. *I knew my grandfather would be a good guy.*

Mr. Smith turned to him with sad blue eyes. "Well, Connor, the truth is, I could have tried harder."

"I didn't exactly make it easy for you, Dad," Connor's mom said. "I should...should have..." She started crying.

"We can talk about 'should haves' all day, Jessica," Mr. Smith said. "We can talk about our regrets. But right now I want to talk about you and my grandson." He nodded toward Connor. "I want to talk about—" He cleared his throat. "I want to talk about what I've missed. It's been a lot of years."

His mother and his grandfather sat and talked for a long time. Connor sat on the steps and let the sound of their voices wash over him like a warm breeze. He wondered if he could come out here for a visit whenever he wanted. *Like a regular kid, visiting his grandfather. Like a normal family.*

Biscuit curled up next to Connor and went to sleep. He stroked her black-and-white fur for a while. She made funny snoring noises. *This could be the next best thing to having my own dog,* he thought.

When it was time to go, Mr. Smith stood up. Connor's mom gave him a quick hug, but the old man looked uncomfortable about it.

"Come by whenever you want," Mr. Smith said. He patted Connor on the back. "You and I have a lot to talk about."

"Can I come tomorrow after school?" Connor asked.

"Connor!" said his mother. She gave him a warning look. "That's too soon. We don't want to wear out our welcome."

"Now, Jessica," said Mr. Smith. "If you don't mind my being blunt, I'm not getting any younger. We've wasted a lot of time." He took off his red baseball cap and slapped it against his leg. "I want to get to know my grandson here. If he wants to come out to the farm tomorrow, that's all right with me. Biscuit and I will be waiting."

Connor grinned. "Okay, thanks...um... Mr. Smith." He almost called him grandpa, but the word got stuck in his throat.

"All right then," the old man said. His face broke into a wide smile.

"Bye, Dad," said Connor's mom. She took a deep breath and said, "Let's talk again soon, okay?"

Mr. Smith nodded and waved, his red cap still in his hand.

Chapter Eight

That night, Connor had the nightmare again. He just expected it now. He had another dream as well, a new one. It was about bees. They were swarming around wooden boxes—manmade hives. Connor could see the weathered gray side of a barn and long grass filled with wildflowers. He felt no danger from the bees, but they kept buzzing louder and louder and louder.

Finally, he opened his eyes and realized that his alarm clock was buzzing. Connor rolled over and smacked it. The noise stopped. He got up and lifted some weights before getting ready for school.

His morning classes flew by. After lunch, biology was canceled, so Connor didn't see

Ashling until English class at the end of the day. She smiled and said hi when he sat down at his desk.

Connor's mind was on his grandfather. He planned to bike over to the little farm after school. *Fifty minutes to go,* he thought, looking at the clock.

"What are you so happy about?" Ashling asked him.

Connor realized that he had a stupid grin on his face. He tried to look a little more serious. "I'm going to visit my grandfather after class," he said casually.

"Oh," said Ashling. "You looked like you just won the lottery or something."

"Well, I just met him for the first time this weekend," Connor admitted. "I didn't even know I had a grandfather before that. So I'm kind of psyched."

Ashling's nose crinkled up in a really cute way. "How come you didn't...I mean... oh, never mind. It's none of my business." Her hair fell forward over her shoulder and she brushed it back with one hand.

Connor tried not to stare. "No, it's okay," he said. "It was just a family fight kind of thing. Something that happened before I was born. It's a long story. But, remember my English story that I told you about?"

Ashling nodded. "The dream story."

"Yeah, well, I based my story on that old man I met out in the country. It turns out that *he's* my grandfather."

Ashling's eyebrows shot up. "That's pretty freaky."

Great, I'm a freak, Connor thought. "Well, that wasn't exactly my dream," he started to say. But then Mr. Lowen came in and started the class, and Connor didn't have time to explain further.

After class, he was eager to get out for his visit. "See you later," he said to Ashling on his way by her desk.

Connor was the first one out the door. Students from other classes were already flooding the hallway, causing a traffic jam. Troy Sellers and one of his football buddies were heading right for the English classroom.

Connor had nowhere to go but forward, so he kept walking. He ignored Troy and picked up his pace. Troy elbowed his buddy as they came closer.

Just as he passed Connor, Troy stepped sideways hard and slammed his shoulder into Connor's. Connor was ready for it, but Troy was a big guy. Connor stumbled from the hit. He managed to get one foot under Troy's, and Troy went down, dropping his notebook.

Connor steadied himself and spun around just as Troy got to his feet.

"Watch where you're going, gentlemen," a voice warned. It was Mr. Lowen.

Troy stepped back. "Sorry, Mr. Lowen. I guess Smith here is a little clumsy," he said.

"Yeah, *whoops,*" Connor said, standing his ground.

"Accidents happen," Mr. Lowen said loudly. "Let's keep the traffic moving." He watched until Troy backed away.

Ashling came out into the hallway and waved to Troy. She hadn't seen a thing.

Connor turned around and started walking for the front doors. All his muscles were tense. *Why did I ever even talk to her?* he wondered. An image of Ashling and her light green eyes popped into his mind. *Oh yeah, I remember now.*

Before long, he was on his bike, pedaling toward River Road. His thoughts turned from Ashling to his grandfather. Connor was looking forward to the visit, but he was nervous, too. *What will I talk to him about?* He didn't know what to expect from a grandparent, since he'd never had one before.

As he sped down the main country road, he saw the hawk. It was sitting on the telephone pole above the stop sign. When Connor got closer, the bird took off. It circled once in the air above Connor, then it flew down River Road toward Mr. Smith's farm.

Connor lost sight of the hawk before he reached the farm. Biscuit came running toward him as he rode up the gravel driveway. She yapped a few times and licked his shoes as he got off his bike.

"Hi, Biscuit." Connor reached down and ruffled the dog's fur.

Mr. Smith was waiting on the porch. "Hello, Connor. I wasn't sure if you'd come." He handed Connor a glass of iced tea.

Connor took a few gulps right away. He'd worked up a sweat biking out here so fast. "Sure, I came. I really wanted to," he said, wiping his mouth.

The old man nodded and took a drink. Connor watched his Adam's apple move up and down in his throat.

"I don't have any other grandparents," Connor blurted out. Then he wished he could take the words back.

"Well, I guess that's partly my fault," said Mr. Smith. His blue eyes looked cloudy and sad. "I can't do anything about your other set of grandparents, and your grandma here died before you were born. But if I wasn't so stubborn, you might have had me around before now. Now, I don't know if you'll even want me."

Connor looked at the wooden floor-boards of the porch. "Yes," he said. It came out kind of husky, and he had to take a drink to clear his throat. "I do," he said, confidently this time.

Mr. Smith reached out and put a hand on Connor's shoulder. "If you and your mom can forgive an old man, then maybe we can make up for lost time."

Connor nodded.

"Now," said Mr. Smith, "how about a tour of the farm?"

"Sure," Connor replied. He followed his grandfather down the steps and across the yard toward a gray barn.

"Not much to see these days," Mr. Smith told him. "The barn's pretty much empty now. My old body can't do what it used to." He waved his hand at the fields that stretched out behind the farmhouse. "The fields are all rented out to the neighbors. I sold some of the land, too. It was just too much to look after."

He pointed at the trees that bordered the driveway. "The woodlot's still mine, though. Andy Burns down the road wants to buy it, but I'm not ready to sell. He might cut it down and build houses." Mr. Smith shook his head. "That just wouldn't be right. A lot of animals have their homes in those trees."

"Like hawks?" Connor asked.

Mr. Smith stopped walking and looked at Connor. He nodded slowly. "That's right, like hawks. I've always been partial to hawks." He looked toward the trees and then started walking again.

They reached the barn. Mr. Smith swung open a huge wooden door and stepped inside. "We used to have cows and pigs in here," he told Connor.

Connor followed him in and waited for his eyes to adjust to the dim light. He looked down a long row of empty stalls. Bits of hay and a lot of dirt lay on the ground. A tiny kitten poked its head around the corner of a stall and came to investigate the noise.

"The only animals in here now are these darn cats," said Mr. Smith. He picked up the kitten in one hand and rubbed its head. The kitten purred loudly.

Connor looked in the stall and saw a large tabby cat lying in one corner. About five kittens were gathered around their mother. Some were feeding.

"Cute," said Connor.

"Well, they keep the mice down," said Mr. Smith. He put down the kitten and led Connor through the barn and out the big door at the back.

Behind the barn, the grass was long and full of wildflowers. Bits of fencing and old tractor parts lay scattered around. A pile of concrete blocks sat near the barn door.

A couple of wooden boxes caught Connor's attention. He walked up for a closer look and stopped short.

They were beehives. Behind a barn.

Just like the ones in my dream.

"Bees," Connor said out loud.

"That's right," said Mr. Smith. "I used to keep bees. I stopped a couple of years ago, though. You know about bees, Connor?"

"No, I just had this dream..." Connor waved his hand toward the old hives.

His grandfather gave him a sharp look. "Dream, huh?"

"Yeah," Connor shrugged. "It was nothing. This just, um, reminded me of it."

"Dreams can be powerful things, you know," Mr. Smith said. He put his hands in his pockets and stared out at the fields. "My mother, that's your great-grandma, she used to talk about dreams a lot. Said they told her things. I don't know about that. But I've been known to have some interesting dreams myself." He looked at Connor. "Must run in the family."

Mr. Smith started walking back toward the farmhouse. Connor hurried to catch up. "Do you think so?" he asked.

"I do," his grandfather answered. "What about you, Connor? What do you dream about besides bees?"

Connor thought about telling the old man about the nightmares. He decided it couldn't hurt. "I've been having weird nightmares lately," Connor told him.

"Is that right?" said his grandfather. "What are they about?"

Connor told him everything—about the dark clouds, the hawk, the spinning and screaming. He told him about the hawk turning into a man who was trying to tell him something. He left out the part about the man being Mr. Smith. *That might sound a bit too weird*, he thought.

"The dreams started right after I met you," he told his grandfather. "Right after I found that hawk feather."

"That sounds interesting all right," said Mr. Smith as they reached the house. He stopped and looked at his watch. "Do you want to come in and do some research or do you have to get home for supper?"

Connor shook his head. "Mom's working late tonight. I don't have to be home right away. What do you mean 'research'?"

Mr. Smith held open the screen door for Connor. "Internet," he said. "Go on in to the living room. It's all set up in there."

"No way!" Connor shouted when he walked into the living room. His grandfather had a computer set up on a big desk by the front windows. There was a huge monitor, two speakers, a CD burner, a scanner, and a color printer. The latest, fastest CPU sat under the desk, humming.

Who knew? Connor thought to himself. *I have a cool grandpa.*

Mr. Smith came in with a large bowl of peanuts. He sat the peanuts beside the keyboard and pulled two chairs up to the desk. He sat down and patted the chair beside him. "Have a seat and let's get to it."

Connor was sure his mouth was hanging open. "This is a pretty good setup you have here," he managed to say.

His grandfather grinned and logged onto the Internet. "This thing is great for keeping an old man busy. I can play bridge with people in England!" He winked at Connor. "I have a high-speed connection," he said proudly.

"Now, let's look up dreams." Mr. Smith started typing words into a search engine. He only used two fingers, but he was pretty quick. "Okay. You said there was a hawk in your dream. I'll try typing in 'hawk dream' and see what we get."

The computer screen filled up with information. "Let's look at this one," his grandfather said, clicking on a link. "Hawk Medicine. That sounds interesting. It looks like a Native American website." He started to read out loud. "It says here: 'In the Native American tradition, "medicine" is anything that brings healing, power, and understanding. It is a way of living in connection with the Earth and all beings. Different animals can bring lessons or medicine to people who have the ability to see them.'"

"What about a hawk?" Connor asked.

"Hm, let's see." His grandfather scrolled down the web page and kept reading. "Oh, here we are: hawks. 'The hawk is a messenger. If a hawk appears in your life, it is a sign. Look for a message that is coming to you. The hawk is also a sign of change or transformation. When the hawk appears in your life, you can expect some interesting changes.'"

"You can say that again," said Connor.

His grandfather chewed thoughtfully on some peanuts. "Well, the hawk flew into your life, that's for sure. So, it must be bringing some kind of message."

"Hey!" Connor said. "In my dream, the hawk turns into a man who is trying to give me a message."

Mr. Smith nodded slowly. "Mmm hmm. Very interesting." He clicked on a link for another Native American site. He read the text that appeared on the screen. "This one says that hawks bring you a message from the universe. And that they help you figure out what the message means. That's what Hawk Medicine is. It says 'Only those with Hawk Medicine can interpret the message and learn the truth.'" He looked at Connor.

"Hawk Medicine," said Connor. The words rolled off his tongue.

"Hawk Medicine," his grandfather repeated softly.

"I don't know," said Connor. "My hawk hasn't helped me figure anything out so far. He's just keeping me up at night."

"Maybe you need to pay a little more attention," said Mr. Smith. "Focus on your dream a little more."

"More!" Connor exclaimed. "I'm trying to focus on it *less* so it will go away!"

"That could be the problem," said his grandfather. "You need to focus on it more and figure out what the message is. Until you do that, I'll bet it won't go away."

"How the heck am I supposed to do that?" Connor asked.

Mr. Smith took another handful of peanuts. "You could try writing down your dreams," he suggested. "I do that sometimes, when I'm having a troublesome dream."

He got up and walked over to a tall bookcase. He took a book from one of the shelves. "You can use this," he said, handing it to Connor. "I'll never use it."

"Cool, thanks," said Connor, running his hand over the smooth brown leather cover. Flipping open the book, he saw that it was full of blank pages.

"Use it every morning when you wake up," his grandfather said. "Write down everything you remember about your dream. Then read it again before you go to bed the next night. Things might start to get clearer."

"It can't hurt to try it, I guess," said Connor, though secretly he had his doubts.

"I'll do some more research," his grandfather told him. He glanced out the window. "It's time you were getting home. I don't want you biking home in the dark."

The sky outside the living room window was streaked with orange. Sunset. Connor reluctantly got ready to leave. He thanked his grandfather, gave Biscuit one last scratch behind the ears, and said good-bye.

As he biked down River Road, he saw the hawk flying up ahead of him. *Are you trying to tell me something, Hawk?* Connor asked silently. *Are you bringing me Hawk Medicine?*

The hawk let out a keening cry and disappeared behind the trees.

Chapter Nine

Connor tried his grandfather's suggestion. Every night, he had the nightmare. Every morning, he wrote down all the details that he could remember.

The scariest part of the dream was the spinning and screaming. After a few days, Connor realized that there was another sound in the dream—a kind of screeching sound. But he didn't know what it was. The hawk still turned into the old man. The man was trying to tell him something, but Connor wasn't getting the message.

He tried sleeping with the hawk feather under his pillow. Nothing.

By the following week, he was feeling frustrated. He was getting nowhere with the dream. *Maybe all this Hawk Medicine stuff is just a bunch of garbage,* Connor thought. *But what if it isn't? What if I'm supposed to be getting a message?*

His grandfather had printed out a bunch of information from the Internet and given it to Connor. Connor read it all, but it didn't help him understand his dream any better. He figured it was time to do some more research. He wondered if the school library had any books on dreams.

Connor went to the library on his lunch hour. It was practically deserted. The librarian was sitting at her desk, reading. The room was silent except for the hum of computers.

A catalogue search didn't reveal much. The computer listed only a couple of non-fiction books on dreams. Connor followed the numbers on the shelves to the very back of the library. The two books were at least fifty years old. When Connor pulled them off the shelf, dust went flying. He sneezed.

A few seconds later, he heard someone else sneeze.

Connor put the books back on the shelf and took a few steps down the aisle. A pair of shoes came into view. Girls' shoes. Connor was about to turn around when the owner of the shoes bent forward. Suddenly, he realized who it was.

He walked to the end of the row. "Ashling?" he said.

She was sitting on the floor, leaning against the end of a bookshelf. There were only a few feet between the bookshelves and the wall. *Oops*, Connor thought, *if she's sitting way back here, she probably wants to be alone.*

Ashling looked up. "Hey," she said with a shy smile.

"Are you okay?" Connor asked. "I mean, do you want me to leave you alone?"

She shook her head. "No, it's okay. I just kind of needed to get away from everyone, you know?"

"Yeah," Connor said. "I know. So I really won't be offended if you tell me to go away."

Ashling laughed. "No, stay. You're good to talk to."

"Really?" Connor sat down opposite Ashling and leaned against the wall.

She nodded. "Really."

"So, who are you trying to get away from? Reesa?" he asked.

"No. She's...I'm fine," Ashling said, blushing. "That was just a stupid thing." She covered her face with her hands, then looked up at Connor. "It's just Troy."

"What's wrong with him?" Connor asked. *Not that I couldn't answer that question myself*, he thought.

Ashling laughed again. "Nothing. I'm just not sure about…you know, going out with him." Her cheeks turned even redder. "I can't believe I'm telling *you* this."

"Why?" Connor wanted to know. "I said I wanted to be your friend. That can include girl stuff." *I'm pathetic*, he thought to himself. *I'm willing to listen to her talk about Troy. This is not good.*

She took a deep breath. "It's not a big deal, he's just being a jerk right now. I like him and everything, I mean, he's nice most of the time. And he's cute."

Connor groaned inwardly. *How did I get myself into this? I don't want to hear this stuff.*

"It's just that he's kind of pressuring me right now," Ashling continued. "And he's being weird about…about who I can be friends with."

Connor waited for her to finish talking. "I don't know what to tell you," he said. *Except to dump the jerk.* "But I think you should be with someone who treats you right."

Ashling sighed. "Yeah, I know." She looked at her watch. "Oops, time for biology. We should go."

Connor stood up and offered Ashling a hand. She took it, and he pulled her up.

"Thanks," she said, letting go of his hand. "Thanks for listening, too."

Together, they walked to the front of the library. A senior student was pinning up a big poster near the front doors. It was for the upcoming dance.

"Hey, look," said Ashling. "Are you coming to the dance next week? You said you weren't sure before."

"I probably won't go," said Connor.

Ashling pointed to the poster. "There's going to be a band."

Connor stepped up to take a look. "Oh, yeah?" *That might not be so bad*, he thought.

She nodded. "We had the same thing last year. A band played for an hour or so, and then the DJ came on."

"Is this band any good?" Connor asked.

"Yeah. They're local, but they're really incredible," said Ashling. "They do some covers, and the lead singer is amazing. You should see all his tattoos. The band does originals, too. The drummer tells jokes and stuff—he's really funny. And the bass player, well…he's awesome."

Connor read the poster. *Maybe I'll check out their website*, he thought.

"Anyway, it's lucky that we got them to play here," Ashling continued. "I think they're going to get a record deal soon. If that happens, they won't be doing gigs at school dances anymore."

"I'll think about it," Connor said.

As Ashling pushed open the door to leave the library, she turned around and looked at Connor. "Well, I think you should come," she said, walking backward out the door.

Connor called out a warning. "Ashling, watch out for—"

She bumped into a group of people standing outside the library. One of them was Troy Sellers.

Troy turned around and glared at Connor. He put his hands on his hips. "You should come where?" he said loudly.

Ashling stepped in front of him. "I was just telling Connor that I think he should come to the dance."

Troy's eyes narrowed.

"Since there's a bunch of us going," Ashling added quickly.

Troy didn't take his eyes off Connor. "Smith," he said, shaking his head slowly. His voice was low. "Didn't I tell you to leave my girlfriend alone?"

Suddenly, Connor was tired of the stupid games. *What's wrong with talking to Ashling? Am I not allowed to have* one *friend?*

"Take it easy, Sellers," he said out loud. "You can drop the tough-guy routine."

Troy took a step forward. "What did you just say to me?"

A crowd was forming. Two of Troy's friends looked at each other and shrugged.

Connor stood his ground. "I said, you can drop the tough-guy routine. I'm not hitting on your girlfriend."

Troy took another step forward. "Well, that's not what it looked like to me."

Ashling grabbed Troy's arm. Troy pushed her away so hard that she stumbled.

Connor lost it. "Hey, watch it," he snapped. He stepped forward and shoved Troy by the shoulders.

Troy hauled back and swung a punch. Connor jumped aside easily. Troy was big, but he wasn't fast.

"Don't tell me how to treat my girlfriend," Troy said. He took another step forward. "I don't need advice from a loser like you." He swung another punch.

Connor ducked and came back with a punch of his own. His fist connected with Troy's face and his knuckles felt like they exploded on impact. He must have hit bone.

Troy swore and tackled Connor. Connor went over backward, and the back of his head hit the tile floor. His vision went cloudy for a second or two. Then he grabbed Troy and tried to roll. The guy was heavy, but he managed it. The two of them started wrestling in the middle of the hallway.

Someone screamed. People started chanting, "FIGHT! FIGHT! FIGHT!"

Suddenly, someone was pulling him up. Connor struggled, but he couldn't shake off the two strong arms gripping his shoulders. He looked over and saw Mr. Lowen restraining Troy. Blood was streaming out of Troy's nose.

Ashling was standing nearby. She had one hand over her mouth.

"I'm all right, you can let go," Connor said to the person who was holding him. It was the vice principal of the school, Mr. Chen.

Mr. Chen let go of Connor. "You two," he said, pointing at Connor and Troy. "My office. Now." His voice was hard and angry.

"Okay, folks, show's over," Mr. Lowen said to the students who had gathered in the hall. People starting walking away, talking to each other in low voices.

Ashling looked at Troy, then at Connor. She shook her head and walked away.

Connor felt like he'd been punched in the stomach, even though Troy hadn't hit him there. *I'm an idiot,* he thought. *And now Ashling knows it.*

Mr. Chen led them down the hall, with Connor on one side of him and Troy on the other. The back of Connor's head was throbbing. His knuckles ached.

The bell rang, signaling the start of afternoon classes. *I guess I'll be missing biology,* Connor thought.

They reached the main office of the school. Mr. Chen pointed to a bench. Connor and Troy sat down as far away from each other as possible.

"Mr. Jameson," said Mr. Chen to the man sitting behind the front desk. "Keep an eye on these two." Mr. Jameson looked over at the two boys and nodded.

Mr. Chen went into the principal's office and shut the door. Connor stared at the closed door for a minute. A little black sign on the door said "Mrs. Greta Steinberg, Principal" in white letters.

Shortly, Mr. Chen reappeared and waved Connor and Troy into his own office. The boys sat down in straight-backed chairs in front of the vice principal's desk.

Mr. Chen sat behind his desk and leaned forward on his elbows. "I don't think I have to tell you two that fighting is a serious offense in this school."

Connor stared at the carpet. It was ugly and gray and scratchy looking.

"The school handbook rules are clear," continued Mr. Chen. "They state that if a student is caught fighting, he will be automatically suspended for one day. Longer, if he is already on a warning. Connor, since this is your first offense, you will be given a one-day suspension."

Connor looked up and nodded.

Mr. Chen cleared his throat. "Troy, this is your first offense this year. You can consider yourself lucky that the principal and I have agreed to clear the slate. You will be suspended for one day."

Troy crossed his arms and slumped in his chair. "Fine," he mumbled.

Unfortunately, Mr. Chen wasn't finished his lecture. "I understand that your little disagreement in the hallway had something to do with the upcoming dance," he said. "I'm sorry to inform you that you will not be allowed to attend the dance. That goes for both of you."

The vice principal gave both boys a stern look. "This school does not condone violence. If it happens again, the consequences will be much worse, I promise you. Is that clear?"

"Yes, sir," said Connor.

"Yes," said Troy.

Mr. Chen stood up and walked toward the door. "Both of you are now on warning status. If you show up at the dance, you will be suspended for one week. If you are caught fighting again, you will be suspended for one week. Please go directly to your lockers, get your belongings, and leave the school grounds immediately. I will see you both back here on Wednesday morning."

He opened the door and held it open for Connor and Troy. "Gentlemen," he said as they left the office. They passed by Mr. Jameson at the front desk and went out to the main hallway.

"Great," muttered Troy. He shot Connor a look. "Stay out of my way if you know what's good for you, Smith," he said in a low voice. Then he turned and walked out the front doors of the school.

Connor walked down the quiet, empty hall to his locker and grabbed his stuff. It felt weird going home this early. He had never been suspended before. His mom probably wouldn't be happy about it.

He biked home. Fortunately, his mom wasn't home, so he didn't have to tell her right away. Connor poured himself a big glass of juice and stretched out on the living room couch. The couch wobbled, and his juice spilled on his jeans.

"Ahhhh!" he yelled, jumping up. He went to the kitchen to grab a towel. Then he went back to the living room and pushed the block of wood back under the short leg of the couch. He sat down carefully, making sure everything was stable.

He lay back on the couch and put a pillow over his head. *This day sucks,* he thought. *It can't possibly get worse than this.*

Unfortunately, it could. The phone rang. It was Ashling. "Are you all right?" she asked.

"I guess," Connor replied. His head and hands ached. "Where are you?" he asked her.

"I'm calling from the pay phone at school. I skipped biology. I already talked to Troy. I know you guys got suspended."

"Oh," said Connor.

"Look," Ashling said, "I'm just calling to say that I know you were just defending me or whatever. So, thanks. But I can look after myself, okay? I'm really not into the whole guy fighting thing."

Connor didn't know what to say. He thought he heard a sniff. "Are *you* all right?" he asked.

Ashling sniffed again. "Yes. No. I'm just mad at you guys, I guess. I hate fighting. I hated watching that."

"Sorry," Connor said. "I'm not into fighting, either. Really. I just lost it when Troy pushed you. And I was getting tired of taking his crap."

"Yeah. Well, I have to go," Ashling said.

"Okay," Connor said. The line went dead.

He stared at the portable phone in his hand. *Way to go, Smith. She's not interested in the 'guy fighting thing.' Like I am. The question is, did she call me because she cared how I was or because she wanted to tell me off for the fight? Seeing as she called Troy first, she probably only called me to tell me off.*

He tossed the phone on the couch and went to his bedroom. There was only one cure for this kind of day. Loud music and drums.

After putting on a CD of the hardest, noisiest rock band he could find, he sat down at his drum set. His hand hurt when he picked up the drumsticks and started playing. It wasn't too bad, though. The drumming distracted him from the pain. It reminded him that there were other things in life besides girls and their stupid football-player boyfriends. Other things besides school and teachers and getting suspended.

Eventually he got hungry. He stopped playing and wandered into the kitchen for dinner. In the fridge, he found a take-out container from the restaurant. It had "Connor dinner" written on the top. Connor opened it and saw a huge piece of lasagna and some garlic bread.

Score, he thought, popping it into the microwave.

After dinner, he studied for a Spanish quiz that he had coming up. Then he had a brilliant idea. *If I'm asleep when Mom gets home, then I won't have to tell her about getting suspended until tomorrow.* He went to bed at nine o'clock.

Connor remembered to read his dream journal before he turned out the light. Random words floated through his mind as he drifted off to sleep. *Clouds. Storm. Danger. Dark. Hawk. Hawk Medicine.*

He woke up in the middle of the night, traces of the nightmare still flashing through his brain. The house was silent and dark. Connor flipped on the light and tried to write down what he remembered. "Hawk. Spinning. Screaming. Screeching noise," he wrote. His eyes were only half open. "Crashing."

Then he yawned and turned out the light. He didn't dream again.

Chapter Ten

Connor's mom knocked on his bedroom door on Tuesday morning at eight. "Connor, honey!" she called from behind the door. "Are you up?"

"No," he groaned. "No school today."

"What do you mean?" His mom opened the door and came in. "Are you sick?"

"Suspended," he said.

His mom's eyes widened in shock. "What? What happened?"

Connor told her the story. He told her everything—about Ashling, Troy, Reesa, the fight, the dance.

She wasn't as upset as he expected. She wasn't happy about it, but she didn't go ballistic. All she did was tell him to clean the bathroom and the kitchen while she was at work. Then she left for the day.

Connor went back to sleep. When he finally got up, he grabbed the dream journal from beside his bed. He took it to the kitchen and read it while he ate breakfast. He went over the details of every dream that he had recorded. The last entry was from last night. He barely remembered waking up and writing down the dream. But there it was: "Spinning. Screaming. Screeching noise. Crashing."

He paused with a spoonful of cereal half-way to his mouth.

Crashing. Something was crashing.

Connor rushed through his chores and then biked out to River Road. His grandfather was surprised to see him, but he shook Connor's hand and invited him inside.

"I think my dream is about something crashing," Connor blurted out. "And people are screaming."

The old man frowned. "Hm," he said, thoughtfully. "Do you know what's crashing?"

Connor shook his head. "Could be an airplane, or a car, or a train. Or maybe it's a bomb or...I don't know."

"I did some more research on the Internet," his grandfather said. "I didn't find much more about Hawk Medicine. But I did find something on dreams." He led Connor into the living room. The computer was on. The monitor showed a spread of cards.

"Hey," said Connor. "My mom plays that game all the time."

Mr. Smith chuckled. "I taught her how to play solitaire when she was a girl. We had to use real cards back then." He sat down and closed the game. Then he opened his web browser and clicked on a bookmarked link.

After the page loaded, he tapped a finger on the screen. "This website talks about working with dreams. It says to sit down in a quiet place and close your eyes. Then try to remember the dream. Have someone sit beside you. Tell them your dream as if you are having it right then." He looked at Connor. "Do you want to give it a try?"

Connor shrugged. "Sure, why not?"

His grandfather pointed to an old leather recliner. "Why don't you sit over there?"

Connor settled himself in the soft chair. His grandfather pulled up a chair beside him. "Okay," he said. "Close your eyes and take a few deep breaths." He waited for Connor to do that, then he said, "Now, tell me your dream. Start at the beginning."

"First, I saw the hawk," Connor began.

"Use the present tense," his grandfather interrupted. "Like the dream is happening right now. So, you'd say 'I *see* the hawk.'"

Connor started again. "I see the hawk. It's flying." He tried to pretend that he was watching the dream as though it were a movie playing on the back of his eyelids. "There were...there *are* dark clouds in the sky, like there's going to be a huge storm. Everything is dark. Now it's starting to spin. It feels like the world is spinning. I can hear screaming...and there's a screeching noise like...like...*tires on wet pavement*."

He sat up and opened his eyes. "It's a car crashing," he said.

Mr. Smith nodded.

"I'm sure that's what it is," Connor said. "I couldn't see it, but I could...feel it." He looked at his grandfather. "So, what does it mean? Is there going to be a car accident? Am I supposed to avoid riding in cars from now on or something?"

"Oh, I don't know," said Mr. Smith. "It could be a metaphor. Like your brain is showing you something, but it really means something else."

"Huh?" said Connor.

"Well, for example, I read on the Internet that if you dream about death, it might just be a sign that you are about to go through some kind of transformation."

"Like transforming from a live person to a dead one?" Connor asked.

"Not necessarily. It could mean any kind of change."

"That's really not very helpful," Connor said, frowning.

Mr. Smith let out a bark of laughter. "Well, that's life, I'm afraid. No easy answers." He patted Connor on the back. "Some people say that dreams are just random nerve activity in your brain and that they don't mean anything. But, in my experience, if a dream keeps coming to you, then it does mean something. If the meaning isn't clear, then you just have to pay attention."

"Pay attention to what?" Connor asked.

"Everything," said his grandfather. "Pay attention to the things going on around you; pay attention to what people say. Watch for things that stand out somehow or seem unusual. They might be clues."

"I'll try, I guess," Connor said.

But as he biked home later, he wondered how he was supposed to do that. *How can one person pay attention to everything?* For the millionth time, he cursed his dream.

After his day of suspension was over, Connor went back to his daily routine. School, work, homework, eating, sleeping, dreaming.

The sounds of the car crash became more vivid in his dream. But he wasn't getting any more clues about the message behind the dream. If there even *was* a message. Still, he kept his hawk feather with him most of the time. Just in case.

Connor tried his best to "pay attention to everything." But he didn't really know what to look for.

That weekend, his mom went out to the farm. Connor wanted to go, but she said she needed some time alone with her dad. "We're still getting to know each other again, Connor. It might take a while."

When she got home, she told Connor that she had invited Mr. Smith over for Sunday dinner in a couple of weeks. She seemed kind of nervous about it, and she asked Connor if he wanted to help her decide what to cook.

At least one thing in my life is going right, Connor thought.

The next week at school, he saw Ashling a lot, but they didn't talk much. An air of tension hung between them. Connor saw that Ashling was avoiding Troy, too. He took some comfort in that, but it didn't last long.

On Thursday, Ashling walked into biology class carrying a red rose on top of her books. She sat down next to Reesa. "Troy finally apologized," Connor heard her say.

Great, Connor thought. *A guy can be a total jerk, but if he gives his girlfriend flowers, she gives him another chance.* He wished he'd thought of the flower thing himself. Not that he would have given her one—she might have got the wrong idea. It just went to show him that he wasn't boyfriend material. He didn't have the right instincts.

After English class that day, Troy was waiting in the hall for Ashling. Connor couldn't get away fast enough.

"I'm still going to the dance tomorrow night," he heard Ashling tell Troy.

"So, I'll pick you up when it's over," Troy's voice boomed down the hall.

Connor walked faster. The idea of changing schools every year suddenly seemed appealing. For the first time in his life, it looked like his mother wanted to stay somewhere. And for the first time, he wanted to leave.

Chapter Eleven

On Friday, Connor tried to ignore the buzz that was going around the school. Everyone was talking about how great the band was going to be.

For once, there's an extracurricular school event that I might want to check out, he grumbled to himself. *But noooooo. I can't go. I had to go and get myself banned. Good one, Smith.*

Connor didn't even have a shift at Dave's Music that evening. That would have taken his mind off the dance.

He biked home after school feeling sorry for himself. He kept imagining what it would be like to be at the dance with Ashling. Maybe even dancing with her. Since it was his own little fantasy, he erased Troy from the scene.

By the time he reached his house, he realized that he was torturing himself. He needed to clear his head. Drumming helped. He put on a CD and let the music run through his head. No words, just sounds.

Later, he ate dinner with his mom. She had plans to go out with Gina for the night, so Connor would have the house to himself. That suited him just fine. He was too miserable for company, anyway.

He washed the dinner dishes and went to his room. He crashed out on his mattress and stared at the ceiling for a while. A gust of wind shook the house. Connor heard the soft sound of rain hitting the window as his eyelids grew heavy, and he slid into a deep sleep.

Ashling was in his dreams. She was laughing with him in the field, and they were watching the hawk together. It was raining. The wet grass was the same color as Ashling's eyes. Lightning zigzagged through the dark clouds overhead.

Suddenly, the world started to spin. Connor reached for Ashling's hand so he could keep her safe. She was too far away. He started to panic. Connor called out, but Ashling was running away from him. She didn't understand the danger, and he knew that he had to warn her. He ran as hard as he could, but she kept running ahead of him.

The world was spinning out of control, and Connor lost his balance. Then everything went dark.

A huge crack of thunder jolted Connor out of the nightmare. He sat up in bed, his heart beating wildly. *Ashling.*

Rain spattered against the window. Connor's sense of panic from the dream was still sharp. He rubbed his eyes. He couldn't shake the feeling of Ashling in danger.

Lightning flashed outside—once, twice. Thunder boomed again a second later. The house was shaking. So was he. *The storm must be right overhead.*

The storm.

Is this the storm I've been dreaming about? It seems a little crazy, but what if it is? And what if Ashling really is in danger? Connor felt a knot of fear form in his stomach.

He thought about what his grandfather had said. *Hawk Medicine. Interpret the message. Pay attention. Pay attention.* Suddenly, in his mind he heard Ashling's voice. "I'm still going to the dance." And Troy's voice. "I'll pick you up when it's over."

My dream is about a car crashing.

Connor jumped out of bed and ran for the door. They might commit him to a mental institution after tonight, but he was not going to let Ashling get in a car with Troy Sellers.

By the time Connor got outside, the rain had stopped. The storm rumbled faintly in the distance. He rode along the quiet streets toward school, his bike tires swishing along the wet pavement.

Ashling is going to think I'm crazy, he thought. But if something happened to her tonight, he would never forgive himself. He had to at least try to talk to her.

Maybe I am actually going crazy. Connor hadn't thought of that angle. *Do crazy people know they're crazy?*

He decided to risk it. *Ashling is already avoiding me, so it can't get too much worse. I'll just go in and talk to her and tell her that she should take a cab home tonight. That would sound pretty reasonable, wouldn't it?*

Then he realized that taking a cab still meant getting into a car. A car that could crash. *Okay, I'll tell her that she should walk home. I'll walk with her. I'll tell her it's an emergency and that I need to talk to her. We can leave before the dance is over, so Troy won't see us.* He just needed to think of an emergency. He decided to make it up as he went along. The important thing was to keep Ashling from getting in a car.

When Connor got to the school parking lot, he heard the low *boom boom boom* of music coming from the gym. Someone had propped open the side doors of the gym with two metal chairs. Connor quickly scanned the cars that were parked in the school lot. Troy's red sports car was nowhere to be seen.

Connor locked his bike to the fence. Then he walked over to the double doors and looked in. The DJ had his equipment set up on the stage. A few kids were lined up at his table, waiting to make song requests. *I guess I missed the band,* Connor thought.

He glanced over his shoulder and then stepped inside the dark gym. Colored lights flashed on and off, occasionally illuminating the huge mass of people dancing in the middle of the room. It wasn't going to be easy to find Ashling. He peered into the crowd.

Suddenly, a deep voice behind him said, "Mr. Smith!"

Connor spun around to see Mr. Chen. *Oops,* he thought. *I should have known someone would be watching the door.*

"I assume you have forgotten that you were banned from this event," said Mr. Chen.

"Uh, yes sir," Connor said.

"Now that you have been reminded, I suggest that you head right back out those doors. Otherwise I will be forced to suspend you for a week. You have exactly sixty seconds to disappear."

"Yes, sir," Connor said again. He stepped back out into the parking lot.

Great. Now how am I going to find Ashling?
Connor walked over to his bike and leaned against the fence. He had a good view of the gym doors. *Maybe Ashling will come out for fresh air at some point. Or maybe she'll leave early.* He knew one thing for certain: he didn't want to try talking to her while Troy was around.

He checked his watch, then rubbed his arms, wishing he had put on a sweater under his jacket. At least it wasn't raining anymore.

A small group of people came outside. Ashling wasn't among them. They walked away from Connor, toward the street. When they reached the edge of the school property, they lit cigarettes and stood around talking.

Other people drifted in and out of the gym doors. After what seemed like hours, the music stopped. Connor looked toward the gym. The DJ's voice drifted out, announcing the last song of the night. A slow song started to play.

A few people came outside, and then a few more. The parking lot started to fill up. Some people stood around talking, some walked to their cars. Finally, Connor spotted Ashling coming out the doors. Reesa was with her. He knew he only had a few minutes before Troy showed up and things got messy. It was time to make a move.

"Ashling!" he called.

She and Reesa turned around as Connor ran up to them. "What are you doing here?" Ashling asked.

"Hi. Hi, Reesa," Connor said, slightly out of breath. "Listen, I was wondering if I could walk you home," he said to both of them.

Reesa laughed. "Whatever. We've got a ride, thanks," she said.

"Please don't drive with Troy tonight," Connor said. "I don't think he's a safe driver."

Reesa laughed again. "What are you, her dad?" she said.

Connor ignored her and looked at Ashling. "I'm serious, Ashling. Walk home with me. I need to talk to you."

Ashling touched his arm. "I really can't, Connor. I'm sorry."

The sound of squealing tires and a car horn came from the road in front of the school. Ashling looked over her shoulder. "Look, Troy's car is coming this way. Please don't let him see you here," she pleaded.

It was too late. Troy's car pulled up beside them. "Smith!" Troy yelled out his open window. "You'd better start running."

Troy's buddy was in the back seat. He leaned forward and nudged Troy. He pointed toward the gym. Mr. Chen and another teacher were standing in the open doorway, looking out at the crowd in the parking lot.

"You won't be so lucky next time," Troy snarled at Connor. Then he leaned over and opened the passenger door. "Come on, girls, get in the car."

Reesa and Ashling walked around the car. Connor followed them. "Ashling!" he shouted. "Don't get in the car!"

Ashling hesitated. She looked at Connor and then at Troy.

Troy sat back in the driver's seat and hit the steering wheel with both hands. "Shut your face, Smith, you loser. Ashling, don't be stupid. Get in the car."

Reesa was already climbing into the back seat with Troy's friend. She left the passenger door open for Ashling.

Ashling put one hand on the car door. "I have to go," she said to Connor. "Please go. Before there's another fight."

"Ashling! Come on!" Troy shouted. "Now or never!"

She quickly climbed into the passenger seat and closed the door.

I'm not going to be able to save her, Connor thought. He walked around to the front of the car and put one hand on the hood. "Ashling, I had a dream about this," he said, looking at her through the windshield. He prayed that she would remember the freaky dreams he'd had lately. It was his last chance.

Ashling's eyes met his. Connor spread his arms in defeat and slowly backed away from the car.

Troy gunned the engine. Ashling yelled something at Troy and reached for the door.

Troy gunned the engine again. Suddenly, the car jumped forward. Troy cranked the wheel and the car swerved to the right. Reesa screamed. Connor leaped out of the way, but he didn't quite make it.

The side of the car just grazed Connor's hip, but it threw him off-balance and knocked him to the ground. He felt his palms skid across the wet pavement as he broke his fall.

The car lurched to a halt and Ashling jumped out. She slammed the passenger door shut. "Troy, you are such a jerk!" she yelled.

She ran over to Connor and knelt down beside him. "Are you okay?" she asked. She helped him sit up.

"Ashling!" Troy was leaning across the car and yelling out the passenger window. "If you don't get back in the car right now, I am leaving you here."

Ashling stood up. "Fine!" she yelled back. "Good! We are *so* over!"

The red sports car screeched out of the parking lot. Connor watched the taillights for a second, then he looked back at Ashling. Tears were running down her face.

"I'm so sorry, Connor!" she said. She picked up one of his hands. His palm was streaked with blood and dirt. "You're hurt!"

"It's okay, just let me get up," Connor said. Ashling helped him stand up. "I'm all right," he said.

A small crowd of people had gathered. They started to move away when they saw that Connor was all right. Connor wiped his hands on his jeans. His palms stung and he felt really stupid. *But at least she didn't get in the car,* he thought. "So, um, can I walk you home now?" he asked Ashling.

She let out a kind of a half-laugh, half-sob. "Sure," she said. "If you tell me about this dream you had."

"You probably think I'm insane," he said. *Probably because I am,* he thought to himself.

Ashling shook her head. "Not insane. A little intense, maybe," she said, laughing. She waited for Connor to get his bike. Then they started walking toward the street.

"I had a dream about a car accident," Connor explained. "I probably overreacted, but I was just…worried about you."

Ashling stopped walking and looked at him. "Thanks," she said shyly. "For someone who only wants to be my friend, you sure look out for me a lot."

"What do you mean—"

His question was interrupted by the wail of a siren. A few seconds later, a police car went racing by them, lights flashing. Then an ambulance flew past.

Connor felt a shiver run down his spine. He and Ashling looked at each other. "Are you thinking what I'm thinking?" Connor asked.

Her face was white. She nodded.

"Can you ride on the handlebars?" he asked her. He hopped on his mountain bike.

"I can try," she said. "Good thing I'm wearing jeans."

She climbed up, and Connor held the front wheel steady. "Put your feet on the mudguard," he said. He started pedaling down the street, slowly at first. Before long, he got the hang of balancing the bike with Ashling on the front. "Keep an eye out for flashing lights," he said.

Ashling looked left and right every time they crossed a side street. They were getting close to the downtown area. Suddenly, she shouted, "There!"

Connor jammed on his brakes. Ashling almost went flying off the bike. A short distance away, the ambulance and two police cars were blocking the street. Their lights were still flashing.

"Let's go," Ashling said. "It's probably not them, but you've got me worried now."

Connor started toward the accident scene. As they got closer, he could see what was on the other side of the police cars.

"That's Troy's car!" Ashling shouted. She looked over her shoulder at Connor. "Hurry up!" she urged him.

Connor pedaled faster.

When they reached the police cars, Ashling jumped off the bike and started running. Connor dropped his bike and followed her. Troy's car was sitting sideways next to a telephone pole. The driver's side was facing them. It didn't have a scratch on it.

"Hey!" A police officer started running after them. "Stay back, please!"

Ashling turned. "I know those people! Where are they?" She grabbed the woman's arm. "Are they okay?" Her voice broke.

Connor put his arm around Ashling's shoulders, and she leaned against him.

"They're all fine," said the police officer. "It's okay. Don't worry." She pointed toward the ambulance, which was just pulling away. "We're just sending them in to get checked out. The driver might have a concussion, but other than that, they're very lucky."

"Are you sure they're okay?" Connor asked. He was thinking about his dream.

"Like I said, those three kids were lucky," said the officer. "If one of them had been sitting in the front passenger seat, it might have been another story."

Ashling gasped and ran around to the passenger side of the car.

"Hey!" yelled the police officer. "I said, stay back!"

Connor quickly caught up to Ashling. She was standing totally still, staring at the side of Troy's car. Connor followed her gaze. The passenger door of the red sports car was completely crushed.

Ashling put her hand over her mouth.

Connor put his arm around her shoulders and felt her tremble.

She turned to look at him. "That could have been—"

"Don't say it," Connor said quickly.

The officer guided them back to Connor's bike. "Your friends are fine. They were just driving too fast and the pavement was wet. It's late. Go home and get some sleep. You can call your friends tomorrow."

Connor picked up his bike. He and Ashling started walking back down the street. Neither of them said a word.

They made it to the end of the street, where there was a little park on the corner. Ashling grabbed Connor's hand and pulled him over to a bench. He dropped his bike and sat down beside her.

"I can't stop thinking about it," Ashling whispered. She didn't let go of Connor's hand.

"Yeah," said Connor. He reached over and touched a tear on Ashling's cheek. Then she started really crying.

Connor put his arms around her and somehow they ended up hugging. He was sitting in a totally uncomfortable position, but he didn't want to move. Ashling was sobbing on his shoulder, but for some strange reason, it felt good.

After a few minutes, she sat back and wiped her eyes with her sleeve. "Sorry," she said. "I'm just…" She shook her head.

"It's okay," he said. "It's probably shock or something."

She stared at him for a minute. "How did you…I mean, your dream…you knew…"

"I don't know," Connor said. He was feeling a little stunned.

Then he remembered something Ashling had said earlier. "Hey, what did you mean when you said that thing about me only wanting to be your friend?" he asked.

There wasn't a lot of light in the park, but Connor saw Ashling blush.

"Just that, you know, you seem to care a lot," she said. "Even though you said that you didn't want to go out with me. You said you only wanted to be friends."

"I never said that."

Ashling frowned. "Yes, you did. After English class that day."

"Oh, yeah," Connor said. "That was after Reesa cornered me in biology class and told me to stay away from you."

He took a deep breath and kept talking. "I figured that she told you that I liked you. As more than a friend. You were avoiding me, and I didn't want you to feel uncomfortable around me. I mean, I never wanted to...I never expected...ahhh." Connor ran a hand over his short hair. He tried again. "I knew Troy is...was...your boyfriend. I never would have tried to get in the way of that."

"I thought Reesa told you that *I* liked *you*," Ashling said. "I thought you told me that you just wanted to be friends because you were so nice and you didn't want to hurt my feelings." She covered her face with her hands. "I felt like *such* a loser."

Connor grabbed one of her hands. "You mean, you liked me?" he asked.

Ashling put her other hand over his eyes. Then she leaned forward and kissed him. Her hand slid around behind his head.

Connor tried to kiss her back, but he had to stop because he was smiling too much. Ashling looked up and smiled, too. Then they were both laughing their heads off.

"It must be the shock," Ashling said, after she'd caught her breath.

Connor put his arms around her, and he felt her shiver. "You're cold," he said. "And it's late. Come on, let's go." He stood up, pulled off his jacket, and handed it to Ashling.

"Thanks," she said. A little electric shock zapped between them as their hands touched. "Oooh!" Ashling gave Connor a funny look. Then she pulled the jacket over her head. It looked way too big on her.

They climbed back on Connor's bike. He was glad to get moving, because now he was really cold. Fortunately, it didn't take long to get to Ashling's house.

Connor biked right up to her front door. Ashling jumped off the handlebars and handed Connor his jacket. "Thanks for the jacket," she said shyly. "And, you know, everything else."

"Sure," he said. He leaned over and kissed her again. "Call me tomorrow," he said.

"Okay," she said, smiling. "'Night."

Connor waited until she went inside, then he started for home. His brain was working overtime. *Am I turning into some kind of psychic?* he wondered. *Or was that just a one-time thing? Will I stop having the nightmare now?*

He really wanted to talk to his grand-father about it, to know what it all meant.

Was this for real? Did I save Ashling's life? Maybe she would have gotten out of the car even if I wasn't there. Was it all just a weird coincidence? Is there such a thing as fate? If there is, can it be changed? Connor shook his head in confusion. *I'm way too tired to be thinking about the nature of the universe right now.*

By the time he got home, he was exhausted and cold. Connor quietly let himself into the house and tiptoed toward his bedroom. Then he realized it didn't matter. There was a light on in his mom's bedroom. He knocked quietly on her door.

The door flew open. His mom rushed out and gave him a hug. "Connor, honey, it's so late. I was worried."

"Sorry, Mom," he said. "Ashling...I had to...I...we..." He couldn't quite wipe the grin off his face.

"Uh huh," said his mom. She smiled and stroked his hair. "I can see that you're okay. We can talk tomorrow."

Connor nodded and stumbled into his bedroom. He collapsed onto his mattress and pulled his blankets over him.

When he woke up the next day, he was still wearing his clothes. Connor looked at his clock and realized that he had slept for twelve hours straight.

And he hadn't dreamed at all.

He reached over beside his bed and picked up the hawk feather. He lay on his back and held the feather up to the sunlight that was pouring in through the window. What was it his grandfather had read to him? Something about the hawk flying into your life and bringing surprising changes.

Connor thought about the changes that had happened in his life. He now had a grandfather, a permanent home, a great job, and a girlfriend.

Hawk Medicine, he thought.

Spirit, universe, fate, coincidence, whatever.

Thank you.

Special Thanks

To the people who took the time to read this manuscript and give me feedback—Sam Turton (especially for all the music), Janet Lewis, Paul Lewis, Ben Kooter, and of course the Tea Leaf Press team!

Thanks also to Bob Holmes and Harriet Geller for their input on the title.